LABEL-FREE
LEARNING

LABEL-FREE LEARNING

Supporting Learners with Disabilities

Charlotte Hendrick Keefe
Texas Woman's University

Stenhouse Publishers
York, Maine

Stenhouse Publishers, 226 York Street, York, Maine 03909

Credits:
Page 38: Brenda Parkes. Copyright © 1986. *Who's in the Shed?* Crystal Lake, IL: Rigby. Used by permission of Brenda Parkes.

Pages 62–63: Adapted from "the retelling profile" from Lesley Mandel Morrow. Copyright © 1988. Retelling stories as a diagnostic tool. *Reexamining Reading Diagnosis: New Trends and Procedures.* Susan Mandel Glazer, Lyndon W. Searfoss, and Lance M. Gentile, eds. 128–149; and
Pia Irwin and Judy Nichols Mitchell. 1983, February. A procedure for assessing the richness of retelling. *Journal of Reading, 26,* 5: 391–396.

Page 84: Donald Keefe. Copyright © 1986. *My First Bike.* Makato, MN: Baker Street Productions. Used by permission of Donald Keefe.

Pages 114, 118: Valerie Meyer and Donald Keefe. Copyright © 1990. *Reading for Meaning: Selected Teaching Strategies.* Mission Hills, CA: Glencoe/McGraw Hill. Used by permission of Glencoe/McCraw-Hill.

Page 115. Donald Keefe. Copyright © 1986. *What Do You Eat?* Makato, MN: Baker Street Productions. Used by permission of Donald Keefe.

Library of Congress Cataloging-in-Publication Data
Keefe, Charlotte Hendrick, 1949–
    Label-free learning: supporting learners with disabilities /
Charlotte Hendrick Keefe.
       p. cm.
    Includes bibliographical references (p. 165) and index.
    ISBN 1-57110-023-7 (alk. paper)
    1. Handicapped children—Education—Language arts. 2. Language
experience approach in education. I. Title.
LC4028.K44 1996
371.9'0446—dc20   95-41497
                                                     CIP

Interior design by Cathy Hawkes
Typeset by Technologies 'N Typography

Manufactured in the United States of America on acid-free paper
99 98 97 96 8 7 6 5 4 3 2 1

FOR DONALD KEEFE

CONTENTS

PREFACE

This book is about children who can learn when they have opportunities to develop their potential. It describes the whole language philosophy of learning and how this philosophy can encourage learning in special education classrooms. I have observed the successful results. Children who because of cognitive abilities or behavior problems were destined to be impaired learners, have become readers, writers, and independent learners.

The most positive aspect of the whole language philosophy is that it allows teachers, as well as children and their parents, to discard stereotypic, deficit labels. From a whole language perspective *all* children are valid learners. How each learns is different, but it is neither better nor less. Each child receives the message that he or she is valued, respected, and celebrated. No one is measured against an arbitrary "average" standard.

In whole-language-based special education classrooms, labels disappear. Negative behavior is reduced, and in its place positive behavior appears—an eagerness to learn; smiling; sharing what has been learned; helping each other; respecting each other; and being self-motivated.

As we struggle with inclusion and what it represents, special education is in flux, but it is my belief that whether children with learning challenges are placed in a mainstream classroom or one designated for special learners, a whole language philosophy is a guiding light that can support them in increasing their literacy in positive and constructive ways.

In this book, I want to share what I have learned about whole language and how it can be used to help "special" learners with obstacles to overcome. Much more can be said, but it is my hope that the information and experiences I offer here will encourage teachers to experiment with the concept of whole language or to expand their existing programs.

ACKNOWLEDGMENTS

This book would not have been possible without the assistance of the many teachers I have worked with who were willing to experiment with whole language. Most of the teachers I mention were my students at Southern Illinois University at Edwardsville. We learned together, but I must say that they taught me a lot, and I hope to share their insights. I have used some of their experiences as examples, but many other teachers I have not been able to mention are also doing wonderful things in their classrooms. To all of them I express my deepest gratitude. They are making a difference to the education of learners with disabilities.

The Learner in "Special Learner"

From 1977 until 1982, I was a teacher of students with hearing impairments, most of whom were profoundly deaf. Working with these students showed me the importance of keeping language whole and drawing on previous knowledge and interests as building blocks for learning. It was during this time that I began to search for a way to teach these junior high and high school students to read for meaning and write sentences that made sense. Their hearing impairment had delayed their language development, and their oral language (via sign language) was much more developed than their written language. When we began working together, they could decode words but comprehend little, and they had trouble writing a grammatical sentence. Like a baby's first utterances, one or two words could mean a variety of things: "Pie Mother" could be "Mother baked a pie," for example, but one would usually have to know more about the context to be able to understand the student's meaning.

In the beginning, the classroom was stocked with workbooks, and at the time, that made me happy. However, it didn't take me long to figure out that when an exercise asked questions about a paragraph they had read, it wasn't necessary for them to read the paragraph to answer them. They were clever students, and most of the questions were fill-in-the-blank. They simply matched the fill-in sentence with the appropriate sentence in the paragraph and determined which word was missing. When I asked them to retell what the paragraph said, they couldn't do it because they hadn't really read the text. So I took away the workbooks and asked them to read. I tested their reading by asking questions that did not involve matching, multiple choice, or fill-in-the-blank. They cried, moaned, and groaned—and so did I.

Along with reading, we worked on oral language development (that is, signing and speaking simultaneously). Every Monday morning students were given time to tell about what they had done on the weekend. Soon I started experimenting with this routine. After all the students had reported their news and the rest of us had asked questions for clarification, I asked everyone to go to the chalkboards at the same time. They were to write down their news and then, one at a time, to read aloud what they had written. Since their written expression was underdeveloped, I focused on rewriting one or two sentences. After we had been doing this for a while, I began to notice tremendous improvement in their writing and reading of weekend news. To me this reflected the powerful connection between oral language, reading, and writing. I started applying this newfound discovery to the rest of the curriculum. We would talk about a subject, and the students would write about it and then read what they had written.

Some of my fellow teachers were exploring process writing through the Oklahoma Writing Project. Although I wasn't asked to attend since I didn't teach "regular" students, I listened intently as my colleagues discussed what they were learning. I observed what they did in their classrooms, asked a lot of questions, and experimented in my own classroom. My students wrote every day in their journals about themselves, their friends, and their families. When we did formal writing, we brainstormed ideas and tried prewriting activities. The results were phenomenal—the students were writing sentences that were almost grammatically correct and, what was most impressive, they made sense. Their stories were humorous and sad, communicating feelings that had perhaps been locked away.

Because of their hearing impairment my students lost out on a lot of incidental learning, so I tried to make what they were learning relevant. I noticed that learning was much easier for them when they were seeking answers to their own questions. Because their knowledge of the world was limited, for example, they often asked about things they had observed at school, in their neighborhood, or on TV. If possible, I would locate the topic in the old set of encyclopedias shelved in our classroom. As I looked up the subject I would talk about how to use an encyclopedia. Eventually, they were able to look topics up without my help and would report what they had discovered. I found it amazing that they could do this so well, since their reading ability was supposedly lower than the reading level of the encyclopedia.

Gradually I began to get a sense of how to teach these students. Their hearing impairment did not inhibit their natural curiosity. They simply needed to see connections between what they were learning and the world outside of school. I wondered, in fact, if their desire for information was greater because their access to it was limited. I had to begin to trust them to learn what they needed to learn, but that was difficult, because special education programs are designed to diagnose and remediate deficits, as outlined in Public Law 94-142 (The Education for All Handicapped Children Act).

APPROPRIATE EDUCATION FOR SPECIAL LEARNERS

P.L. 94-142, passed in 1975, was reauthorized in 1990 as the Individuals with Disabilities Education Act (IDEA). This powerful piece of legislation defines categories of disabilities and guarantees free and appropriate education for those who meet specific criteria. The approach is systematic: an assessment determines students' strengths and weaknesses; an individualized education program (IEP), which states annual goals and short-term objectives, is developed; learning tasks are sequenced so that students will be able to meet the stated goals and objectives; and students are assessed annually to determine if they have met goals and objectives. A continuum of services—that is, a variety of educational placements for children who are eligible for special education—are provided and typically range from the most "normal" setting, the mainstream classroom, to resource rooms, self-contained classes, day schools, and residential placements.

P.L. 94-142 was the culmination of years of struggle for the educational rights of children with disabilities, and its enactment promised free and appropriate public education for all children. Almost since its passage, however, the dispute about what is "appropriate" has continued, and throughout the 1980s the system of special education was under attack. Critics have claimed that it is a second system of education, and some have called it inferior and segregationist, while others have complained that the resources for special education should be shared by everyone, not just a few. There have been calls for change: for example, a merger of special and regular education (Stainback and Stainback 1984); full integration of any and all into regular classes, regardless of condition, disability, fragility, vulnerability, or need (Bilken et al. 1985); and a partnership between regular and special education (Will 1986).

The struggle for systemic change was based largely on the perception that services for students were fragmented, that the educational needs of children with disabilities and "slow" learners were not being met, and that labeling and categorizing emphasized failure rather than prevention (Will 1986). According to this perspective, most of the students being served by special education should not be labeled as handicapped (Lilly 1986; Shepard 1987).

The perceived need for systemic change produced the Regular Education Initiative (REI). This was basically a call for a merger of general and special education that would support collaborative efforts to more adequately meet the needs of children with disabilities who have difficulty in school but do not qualify for special education services. For the most part, REI focused on students with mild disabilities and those at-risk for school failure.

Criticism of special education continued. The National Association of State Boards of Education (NASBE), for example, reported that there were two outstanding reasons for poor special education outcomes: the unnecessary segregation and labeling of children for special services, and the ineffective practice of mainstreaming (NASBE 1992).

Eventually, a more radical idea for systemic change came to the forefront—inclusion—yet what inclusion means has been inexact. According to the *Inclusion Times* (September 1993) "inclusion" is the philosophical stance that education should be one unified system in which *all* students (including those with severe disabilities) are legitimate members. It should not be treated as a synonym for "integration" or "mainstreaming" because: mainstreaming and integration evolved from two separate systems, regular education and special education, and there is an underlying assumption that members of the "lesser" system (special education) may join the mainstream (regular education) if it seems possible that they can achieve some type of competence.

Some have made a distinction between inclusion and "full" inclusion. Rogers (1993), for example, defines inclusion as "the commitment to educate each child, to the maximum extent appropriate, in the school and the classroom he or she would otherwise attend" (p. 1), while O'Neil (1993) describes full inclusion as "a concept that, in effect, does away with the option of placing students with disabilities anywhere but in regular classrooms in their neighborhood school" (p. 1).

Proponents claim that inclusion will allow students with disabilities to become better prepared to live in contemporary society and provide more opportunities for communication among students, their peers, and their families. This, in turn, will allow nondisabled individuals to be more aware of and more sensitive to individual diversity (Demchak and Drinkwater 1992; Sullivan and Lewis 1990).

Yet the idea of inclusion also evokes many concerns: general education is not prepared to educate all learners with disabilities (Martin 1994); teachers may not receive adequate support (O'Neil 1993); children with disabilities will not receive appropriate education in general education classrooms (Lieberman 1992); children who are nondisabled will not receive adequate attention (Rogers 1993); and inclusive schools may actually cost more (Council for Exceptional Children 1993).

Because educators and parents fought long and hard for special classes and services in public schools, professional educational organizations have positioned themselves on opposing sides. The Council for Exceptional Children, the Council for Learning Disabilities, and the National Joint Committee on Learning Disabilities are opposed to full-time placement of all students in a general education classroom. These organizations share the belief that the continuum of educational placements mandated by P.L. 94-142 must remain available. On the other side, the Association for Persons with Severe Handicaps, the National Association of School Boards of Education, and the Council of Chief State School Officers have endorsed full inclusion. Those in favor of full inclusion believe that special education as we know it today has not lived up to its promise, and that the continuum should be abolished.

Since inclusion refers mostly to *where* students with disabilities will be educated, it is, in a sense, an "ownership" issue. Advocates believe that individuals with disabilities should be considered "legitimate" members of the mainstream (the regular classroom) and should not have to meet certain criteria before they can participate. Many advocates feel that the quality of education of students with disabilities will be enhanced because they are being exposed to higher levels of learning and better models for language. On the other hand, opponents of inclusion feel that learners who have significant difficulty with learning may not receive appropriate support in a regular classroom and therefore will not reach their maximum potential.

IDEA does not use the term "inclusion," and the Department of Education has not defined the term. However, the law does require school districts, to the maximum extent appropriate, to educate students with disabilities, using supplementary aids and services, in the regular classroom of the school they would attend if they were not disabled. Supplementary aids and services can include modifications to the regular curriculum, the assistance of an itinerant teacher, computer-assisted devices, notetakers, and the use of a resource room (Heumann and Hehir 1994).

According to Susan Stainback and William Stainback (1992), an inclusive school has a sense of community, whereby students and staff support each other; it is a place where diversity is valued; it has a natural proportion of students with disabilities and avoids centers of cluster sites for disabilities; it brings services to the general education class and they are not based on categorical labels; it fosters interdependence in the form of supportive relationships; it integrates special educators into general education as teachers, consultants, support facilitators, and resource locators; it adapts curriculum when necessary; and it combines the resources of special education and general education.

Lieberman (1992) also believes that inclusion calls for individualism, which necessitates child-centered education. Unlike the idealistic inclusion advocates, however, he believes individualism "is on the run." In other words, schools and state governments are mandating arbitrary standards, grade-level expectations, competency tests, and set curriculum. Given the current educational climate, Lieberman concludes that the special education continuum of services must be kept intact. Likewise, Douglas Fuchs and Lynn Fuchs (1994–95) emphasize that the individualization in special education, which is not just permitted but mandated by law, contrasts with the one-size-fits-all approach in many general education classrooms.

What scholars on both sides of the inclusion debate seem to be saying is that we must view "appropriate education" as that which truly meets the needs of individual learners from each learner's perspective. This means we should not try to fit all learners into a standard box and measure their worth by how well they fit. Nor should we dictate instruction according to a label that identifies a specific disability.

From a child-centered perspective, appropriate education means a curriculum, centered in meaningful events, that allows children to learn about their world as they are learning to read, write, and calculate. The curriculum is individualized because learners are allowed to develop from where they are and not rushed through an artificially designed curriculum with preset skills in a specific sequence. A child-centered curriculum allows learners to join the game of learning at their own level. It does not penalize them for a lack of general knowledge but applauds them for what they already know. It frees children to feel good about themselves.

A curriculum based on the whole language philosophy meets these criteria. Whole language is a comprehensive philosophy about learning, about teaching, and about children. The concept expresses a global view of education that considers and addresses the uniqueness of the individual child. It recognizes that their uniqueness comes from their cultural and community heritage, their experiences, their socialization, and their own innate abilities. It also recognizes that before they even begin their formal education, children have learned a great deal of information, and that children who do well in school, children who have difficulty, and children who are placed in special programs all come to school with the ability to learn. The mainstay of whole language is that we accept children as who they are and allow them to continue learning by offering meaningful opportunities to explore and experiment.

LET'S REMOVE THE LABELS

In a whole language classroom children are not considered disabled or deficient. They are viewed in terms of growth. Let me illustrate by describing two primary special education classrooms. Both classrooms include children who have been identified as educable mentally retarded, learning disabled, and communication disordered. The teachers in these classrooms, however, state that these labels have no relevance. One teacher remarked, "Somewhere in my paperwork the children are identified according to a disability, but I don't pay attention to these labels." When I asked the other teacher about how the children in her classroom were classified—mentally retarded, learning disabled, she smiled and said, "I call them first graders." Her students are doing the things other first graders are doing. Both teachers confidently reported that their students were learning to read.

In another school, two children with disabilities are included in a general education classroom. When I asked the teacher to compare these children with other children in her class, she paused a moment and then replied that all of her students are similar: they come to school expecting to learn, and they do learn; and each is unique in that they approach learning in their individual way. The students who have been identified as having a disability are the same as the others—they expect to learn and they do learn in their own individual way. These teachers work in different communities, but they share common ground. They have been influenced by the whole language philosophy.

Often teachers convey the message, "Trust me. I know what you should learn, when you should learn it, how you should learn it, and why you should learn it." Whole language teachers, however, are listening to their students: "Trust us," they say, "we want to learn, and we will learn. Follow our lead." It is human nature to categorize and label. I do not expect that we will stop labeling individuals with disabilities—we have been doing it throughout the ages. As educators, however, in Nicholas Hobbs's words, we should look "beyond definitions, beyond categories, beyond labels, and examine the needs of individual children . . . break away from the familiar but inadequate solutions manifested in current arrangements for exceptional children" (1975, pp. 181–182).

In this book I present actual special education teachers, their classrooms, and their students. The teachers I describe have moved or are in the process of moving the instruction in their classrooms from an efficient, systematic, deficit-driven curriculum to a child-centered, holistic one.

As I have noted, the "inclusion" of special education children in general education classrooms is being discussed and debated. The special education teachers who are watching their students find success through a whole language approach sometimes view inclusion with trepidation. Why? Not because they don't believe their students should be accepted as legitimate members of the educational community, but because they fear that the labels, which have disappeared in their classrooms, will pop up again in a general education classroom that is assessment- and curriculum-driven. They search for ways to provide a child-centered learning environment within a learning community that views all students as legitimate members. Some special education teachers use resource time to make modifications. Rather than tutor or concentrate on remediation of deficits, they use a whole language approach. Some have been able to find whole language cohorts in the mainstream with whom they can collaborate. In other situations, teachers work with students in more self-contained environments to give them time to develop enough literacy skills to feel confident in the mainstream classroom. These teachers have been able to work within the system imposed upon them, but they use the whole language philosophy as a guide to support their students' literacy, their independence, and their confidence that they are indeed legitimate members of a literate community.

This book attempts to explain the whole language philosophy and how it can be applied to "special" learners. I hope that it will encourage all educators to take a few risks and to trust all students to learn. I chose my examples not because they did or did not embrace the so-called inclusion movement, but because they illustrated how far learners identified as having disabilities can progress when a child-centered philosophy such as whole language is in place.

What Is Whole Language?

Whole language is a learner-centered philosophy, a set of beliefs about how children learn language, the role of language in the classroom, and the role of the teacher. The essence of the whole language philosophy is that learning is easy when it is meaningful and pertinent to our lives. This idea is a development of the teachings and research of many philosophers, educators, and researchers from the nineteenth century to the present—among them, John Amos Comenius, John Dewey, Sylvia Ashton-Warner, Jean Piaget, L. S. Vygotsky, Noam Chomsky, Donald Holdoway, Emilia Ferreiro, Ana Taberosky, Kenneth Goodman, Yetta Goodman, Jerome Harste, Michael Halliday, and Brian Cambourne. By observing children as they learn to read and write, we have discovered that children learn to read and write best under conditions that are similar to those in learning to speak: moving from whole to part in contextually meaningful and purposeful settings. We have realized that language learning is simultaneously a social, conceptual, and linguistic process involving the supersystem of conventions that governs all the interactive social, conceptual, and linguistic contexts.

Reflecting on how a baby learns language is a good introduction to the concept of whole language. When learning the cultural conventions of a language, a baby watches everyone and everything, and begins to develop an understanding of the power of speech. Crying doesn't have to remain the generic mode of communication. Sounds can have meaning, and when they have meaning, good things can happen: specific needs and desires are met. The baby therefore experiments with sounds in order to get a response, learning quickly that much attention can be evoked by producing the right sounds. These sounds become meaningful as the baby learns to communicate its needs, to express its feelings, and to be social.

We all know that a baby does not begin to talk using whole adult sentences, but a baby does talk in whole and meaningful utterances. The single word *cookie,* for example, takes on a variety of different meanings, depending on the situation. It can mean "I want a cookie," "I dropped the cookie," "Puppy has my cookie," or "Do you want to share my cookie?" Now it is the parent's (or listener's) turn: time for translation. Experienced language users are very adept at this type of translation. They analyze the utterance in the context of the whole situation and make sense out of it. If the child is looking toward a plate of cookies and pointing toward the plate while uttering "cookie," it is easy to figure out that she wants a cookie.

The development of language, therefore, is a social event. Language is not acquired simply through imitation; it is learned through interpretation. The literacy event that at first appears to be imitative is actually based on an intent to make meaning within the social context (Harste, Woodward, and Burke 1984). Children's oral language develops rapidly as they hear and use language that is functional and purposeful in their natural environment.

EMERGING LITERACY

Reading and writing develop much like oral language. Whole language theory recognizes that listening, speaking, reading, and writing are all language processes that emerge and develop interdependently, each informing and supporting the other. While children are learning about oral language, they are also exposed to the world of print. They are read to; they are given crayons for drawing and pencils for writing. They learn that print on book pages means words, and they begin experimenting with their own reading and writing, much as they did with oral language.

If a child's babble has meaning to the child, so do beginning experiments with reading and writing. Children pretend to read by pointing to words in a book as they make up a story. A child's first scribbles also have meaning. L. S. Vygotsky (1978) believed that the crucial point in written language learning occurs when intended meaning is represented by marks on paper, which act as the placeholders for intention. The scribbles, in other words, are the child's intentional representations for the words they want to write.

Experimenting with reading and writing is a whole process. Children read and write whole stories that make sense to them; they don't read and write sounds. Like oral language, then, written language emerges from a natural desire to communicate, and to do so in whole meanings, not in abstract bits and pieces. Because this natural process is already in place, formal education should build on the knowledge children have already acquired by proceeding in the same manner. Language that is whole and meaningful to children should not be reduced to random pieces when they enter school. In Kenneth Goodman's words,

> Language is inclusive, and it is indivisible. Whole language teaching recognizes that words, sounds, letters, phrases, clauses, sentences, and paragraphs are like the molecules, atoms, and subatomic particles of things. Their characteristics can be studied, but the whole is more than the sum of the parts. If you reduce a wooden table to the elements which compose it, it is no longer a table. The characteristics of carbon, hydrogen, and some other bits may be studied and so help us understand how a table can be, but we don't build a table with them. (1986, p. 27)

This sense of emerging literacy contradicts the traditional view, which compares what children do with what adult readers and writers do. According to Lea McGee and Donald Richgels (1990), the "traditional" mature reader is someone who recognizes words or sounds out words; understands sentences and texts and finds or infers themes; knows the alphabet; and can spell and write. Therefore, children are considered knowledgeable about literacy only when their reading and writing approximates that of adults. In addition, reading requires readiness skills, and writing is learned only after reading. The traditional view of literacy implies that learning to read and write is difficult. But reading and writing do not have to be difficult if they are presented in a meaningful way and if children are encouraged to use language for their own purposes.

WHOLE LANGUAGE PEDAGOGY

The whole language approach to language development is not simply an esoteric set of beliefs. It has influenced the applied pedagogy of classroom teachers, who have in turn contributed further depth and breadth to the theory. Since the essence of the theory is meaningful and purposeful contexts, the classroom learning environment incorporates functional language use to the greatest degree possible. Whole language teachers try to create what are known as "authentic learning events." What this means is that teachers recognize the difference between language (oral or written) used for real purposes and language exercises, no matter how cute or clever.

In order to distinguish between authentic language use and language exercises, it is useful to examine the linguistic subsystems—phonological, syntactic, semantic, and pragmatic. The phonological subsystem is made up of phonemes, the sounds of spoken language. The grammatical rules for combining words to make sentences are the syntactic system, and the semantic system conveys the meaning of words and sentences. Our social use of language is governed by what linguists refer to as the pragmatic system. These linguistic subsystems operate in concert to provide the information from which we construct meaning. When we listen, we hear whole words (not individual sounds), which are part of whole sentences, which are part of a whole thought. We make sense out of what is being said by applying the rules we have learned about conventional grammatical patterns, our knowledge of semantics, and the context. Likewise, when we speak, we use the same set of internalized rules to express our thoughts. These systems, working interdependently, make language predictable (Smith 1971).

Written language (reading and writing) uses the same linguistic systems. By analyzing the mistakes ("miscues") children make during oral reading, Kenneth Goodman (1969) discovered that we use the same linguistic knowledge to construct meaning and make predictions with print that we use with oral language. In written language we use the graphic system, a representation of letters, and the graphophonic system, which informs us about the relationship between spelling and sound patterns. As readers we don't sound out every word; we read only enough to confirm what we expect based on our syntactic, semantic, and pragmatic knowledge of language.

We also use all our cueing systems to figure out words we don't know. Take, for example, the sentence "The tired and hungry boy ate his ham and cheese sandwich in two bites." Let's say that a reader is not familiar with how the word *sandwich* looks in print. The reader can make an accurate guess by activating the cueing systems. The first letter *s* tells the reader what sound the word begins with. The syntactic cues say that word will be a noun, and the semantic cues say that it will be something to eat that has "ham and cheese" on it. In addition, the pragmatic cues help the reader understand the intentionality of the writer's message; a good guess, therefore, will be "sandwich," which makes sense. Even if the reader guesses "snack," the meaning of the entire text is only minimally changed. In the same way, writers use the linguistic subsystems and the aspect of predictability as they create, read, and revise their own texts. Writers must employ appropriate cues so that readers will understand their meaning.

Carole Edelsky (1991) explains that classroom language activities are authentic when all of the linguistic cueing systems are activated. But an activity becomes an exercise when students do not have the opportunity to take advantage of the systematic processing of cues. Reading words from a flashcard is not real reading; it is an exercise because there are no syntactic, semantic, or pragmatic cues to help predict what the word is. Other exercises include filling in blanks on worksheets, writing spelling words five times, or writing a contrived story focused around assigned spelling words. These types of exercises do not allow learners to use language as a whole; rather, they fragment language. Authentic language use in the classroom might be reading a novel for entertainment, writing a letter to the cafeteria supervisor to complain about the food, or using the dictionary to find the meaning of a word in a magazine article. These are authentic language activities if they serve the purpose of the individual pursuing them.

THE WHOLE LANGUAGE APPROACH AND TRADITIONAL APPROACHES

Whole language is not an effort to put a new "spin" on the traditional curriculum. It is based on a different theory of how children learn. The traditional curriculum derives from a reductionist paradigm, which says that we learn a complex act by breaking it down into small pieces and then progressing toward more complex activities. The extremely complex process of learning to read is first broken down into identifying abstract letters, then combinations of letters along with phonics rules. Thus, reading becomes a simplistic task of recognizing letters and the sounds those letters represent. Since words are a combination of letters, all one must do is understand the graphophonic rules (the symbol-sound relationship) and one can break the code and pronounce the word. Curriculum materials usually include basal readers with a controlled vocabulary (which matches the instructional sequence of phonics rules), accompanying workbooks, and other types of practice exercises.

A traditional approach emphasizes the practice of skills over actual reading. Richard Anderson and his colleagues (1985) examined the actual amount of time spent doing "real" contextual reading. In one primary class silent reading occupied seven to fifteen minutes per day; in the middle grades, fifteen minutes per day. Up to 70 percent of the time allocated for reading was spent on related reading activities, such as worksheets or isolated phonics training, or in waiting for directions or for a turn. Students who are subjected to a curriculum like this often consider reading as "doing nothing" or as something they detest. One special education teacher who chooses to have students actually read, rather than use a skills approach, was asked a telling question by a student: "What kind of teacher are you anyway—all we ever do is read!" In another special education classroom, after the teacher announced that the class was going to be spending a great deal of time reading, a student was overheard saying, "Oh yuck, I just hate doing fill-in-the-blank worksheets."

There has been a longstanding debate about the superiority of learning to read by the phonics method or the whole word method. Whole language is often confused with the whole word method, but the only thing they have in common is the word "whole." The whole word method is different from the phonics method, but the approach is still reductionist. Students learn to recognize a lot of words, which are then strung together into sentences. Sometimes the words have the same ending, and only the beginning sound is changed: fan, can, Dan, Nan, pan. When students are able to recognize these words, they can read a sentence: "Dan can fan Nan with a pan." The whole word approach also uses basal readers with worksheets and drills. It is just a variation on a theme: reading as word recognition.

Finally, traditional curriculum gives evidence of achievement through a positivist approach. In other words, curriculum designers decide in advance what students should learn and in what order. Then, they determine students' progress through tests of knowledge and skill application (Keefe 1993).

Whole language theory, in contrast, says that reading is a meaning-making act. We read for a purpose; we expect what we read to make sense. We use prior knowledge to bring meaning to the text. Reading is a social event: the reader interacts with the author's message.

In addition, whole language recognizes that reading and writing are complex activities. As we have seen, it relies on all the subsystems of the linguistic system to provide information about the meaning and construction of text. Frank Smith (1985) and other psycholinguists believe that the meaning of a text is in our heads; it does not emerge from isolated letters or isolated words out of context. In other words, our background experience, our interest in the subject, and our prior knowledge of the subject give us a jump start. With all of this in our heads, we are able to make predictions and make meaning out of the text. A reductionist approach to reading, however, relies almost exclusively on the phoneme system. As a result, learners taught through this approach loose out on important linguistic cues; reading becomes hard.

Brian Cambourne (1982) conducted a study to examine how students with reading disabilities (including students labeled as learning disabled) read. Although the reading-disabled students were limited in their ability to process written text as grammatical and meaningful, they were able to perceive and respond to letter-sound relationships as well as more effective readers. According to Cambourne, although "it could be argued that the proficient group of readers may have a more highly developed semantic and syntactic control of the language, it should be remembered that the reading disabled children's oral language never degenerated to the depths of semantic or syntactic nonsense that their reading language did" (p. 66). The disabled group read material that was less semantically and syntactically demanding and were confused about where to put their effort while reading. Since graphophonic matching requires so much effort, it is difficult for the students' working memory to monitor what they are producing so they can decide if what they are reading makes sense. Therefore, one could argue that a reductionist approach that is designed to make learning easier by reducing the learning task to small segments actually makes learning more difficult.

An educational system based primarily on a reductionist approach carries two messages: 1) Learning is hard; 2) Teachers need all the help they can get. Reductionist approaches and methods include:

- sequenced curriculum determined by external "experts"
- structured textbooks
- drills and exercises
- skills irrelevant to the world outside of school
- emphasis on memorization
- deemphasis on creative thinking
- testing for competency in skills
- external rewards
- discouragement of collaboration
- mastery of discrete information

Pedagogy based on whole language theory reflects a different philosophy: 1) Learning is easy; 2) Students and teachers, as primary participants, are in control of the learning environment.

Whole language classrooms include:

- child-centered curriculum (derived from children's interests and talents, not deficits)
- respect for each individual's culture, experience, knowledge, and skills
- collaboration
- print on display and available
- opportunities to use reading and writing for meaningful purposes
- centers that reflect learners' interests
- good literature
- teacher demonstrations
- an emphasis on students' taking responsibility for their own learning
- a community of learners
- a holistic view of language
- skill-learning through purposeful activities
- a view of errors as markers of growth

WHOLE LANGUAGE FOR SPECIAL LEARNERS

Whole language theory recognizes that students are always learning. Yet obviously some students do not learn in school, and Mary Poplin (1988) suggests five reasons: developmental unreadiness; inactive teaching techniques; insufficient previous and current experiences; insufficient interest; and a mismatch of previous experiences.

Her list can apply to students who are eligible for special services and have been formally labeled as well as to students who have been informally labeled (those students ineligible for special education but not reaching set performance standards). By applying the principles of whole language theory, teachers can create a learning environment in which all learners can thrive:

1. *Developmental unreadiness:* whole language teachers accept the fact that their students are at different stages of development and learning. Because they expect all students to learn, therefore, no students are "unready."

2. *Inactive teaching techniques:* whole language teachers strive to engage students. Cambourne (1988) uses as an analogy the engagement of a clutch before a manual transmission car will move. The engagement of the clutch is the connecting power of the motor that sets the vehicle in motion. In the same way, no matter what teachers do, without the learner's engagement, learning doesn't take place. Whole language teachers strive to give demonstrations that students can perceive as "doable" and "owner-able": they must believe they can do it and that there is a purpose for doing it.

3. *Insufficient previous and current experiences:* whole language teachers immerse their students in meaningful learning experiences, not trivial drills and redundant worksheets.

4. *Insufficient interest:* whole language teachers discover what interests their students and encourage them to explore these interests. These become the focal point for the learning and application of literacy skills, mathematical skills, organizational skills, and social skills.

5. *Mismatch of previous experiences:* whole language teachers strive to keep learning whole. They connect new learning experiences to previous experiences rather than present information in disjointed and isolated pieces.

An eleven-year-old friend of mine exemplifies how dramatically performance can change when whole language principles are applied. He has been through a traditional curriculum in both general and special education in school, but he can barely read a book written on the second-grade level, and it is obvious that reading is torture: he stumbles, he hesitates, he puts his hand on his forehead, he wrinkles his face. Outside of school, however, he pursues his interest in baseball. He reads the sports page every day to find out how his favorite team, the St. Louis Cardinals, is performing. He finds out about runs, hits, errors, and batting averages. Perhaps he doesn't read the sports articles with the same ease as nondisabled readers, but he does read purposefully and with enthusiasm. He views this activity as owner-able and doable. But for him, reading the sports page doesn't count as "real" reading. Real reading is the hard stuff he has to do in school.

For learners with special needs, the guiding principle for a holistic curriculum is the development of language within the context of their needs (Yellen and Blake 1994). It must be kept in mind, however, that these learners have needs beyond those of nondisabled learners, which may require specific adaptations and modifications. A child with a visual disability may need large-print material. Children with physical disabilities become fatigued more quickly. Curriculum planning should consider the time of day in scheduling certain activities; more complex mental activities may need to be interrupted with some that are less fatiguing. Children with learning disabilities may need to observe more demonstrations and be given more time to practice and develop skills.

The whole language philosophy provides a framework for learner involvement and for a curriculum that is child centered and whole. It does not do away with teacher guidance. The teacher continues to make decisions about how to encourage the learning of individual students. For instance, some children have the ability to "take off" on their own, and the teacher may feel that allowing them freedom to do so is the best approach. On the other hand, students with disabilities may need clear, specific demonstrations, opportunities for practice, and feedback that supports their continuous progress toward controlling their own learning. Expectations for individual students are based on the information about what each learner can do.

I have visited the special education classrooms of numerous teachers who use whole language as their guidepost to create a child-centered learning environment. Without fail, I am showered with testimonies of success from children who had at one time been "written off." During my visit to one classroom, a six-year-old boy walked up to me with his hand extended and a broad smile across his face. "Hi! My name is Michael, and I can read and write!" His confidence left no doubt in my mind about his reading and writing ability. I observed him and his peers for the rest of the day. Indeed, they were all readers and writers. The teacher told me that when Michael was in preschool, his mother had been told he would never learn to read and write. Now his mother laughingly reports that he reads everything—even things she doesn't want him to!

In another classroom I observed a group of ten-, eleven-, and twelve-year-olds reading poetry selections. I was intrigued by a boy who read his poem with wonderful vocal and facial expression. The teacher was especially pleased with his progress because he was virtually unable to read when he came into her classroom. Later, she told me that she had asked the school psychologist to test him because she didn't believe his reported intelligence quotient of 40 could be accurate. He was tested and his score was the same—40. The teacher was disappointed that his IQ had not changed, but when she related this story to me, all kinds of thoughts flew through my mind, mainly about the validity of intelligence tests. Finally, I said, "His IQ based on that test may be 40, but he is learning to read and write, so that must mean that you are a wonderful teacher."

One of the more exciting aspects of the whole language philosophy is that its insights into children's learning have actually been put into practice in the classroom. Teachers often complain that theory is mostly esoteric, unrelated to "real" children in "real" classrooms. But in whole language classrooms theory has become not only a related part but an integral one. Teachers who make instructional decisions based on a whole language philosophy do so because they have seen positive results, and they are more confident about what they are doing. We have realized, however, that we cannot accept something just because it "feels good," and we continue to validate our decisions through classroom-based research.

Goodman (1989) points out that whole language research is much broader than typical clinical controlled studies because it takes place in actual classrooms while children are in the actual process of learning. Whole language researchers must take into account the purpose of whole language in their research design. They cannot simply examine the effectiveness of a series of reading or writing strategies but need to be aware of the contextual meaning of what they are measuring. As Goodman illustrates, if researchers intend to evaluate "time on task" in a whole language classroom, then they should have a definition of "task"—such as learner choice, problem solving, and the dual curriculum of linguistic and cognitive development—that fits the concepts of whole language. A better concept to evaluate, he suggests, is learner commitment and involvement. Research is a validating process, but it must be carried out in a manner that reflects the true nature of whole language classrooms.

Teachers who are in the midst of redesigning their classroom and curriculum to reflect a whole language philosophy may find it useful to be familiar with research supporting its efficacy. Being able to discuss such research with administrators, colleagues, and parents can be beneficial. (The Appendix gives a review of selected research, in both general and special education settings, which presents positive results of whole language based instruction.)

IN CLOSING

Those who teach special learners should first expect that they will learn and then trust that their learning will be about what is relevant and meaningful to them. When I present this idea to teachers, they ponder it and then reply, "Yes, but . . . they may not learn what is on the curriculum objective list and within the time frame that is required." Then I ask, "Do your students normally meet the curriculum objectives within the specified time frame?" Without much hesitation they reply, "No . . . the end-of-the-year conferences are so frustrating. According to test scores they've made little progress." Next I suggest, "Then why not try something different? Let your students choose what they want to learn, read what they want to read. If it doesn't work, what will be lost? Take a risk."

The whole language philosophy views learning as a natural, ongoing process. It recognizes that we learn all the time, and that learning is not difficult when it is relevant to our purposes. It also recognizes that all children can learn if they are respected for who they are, where they come from, how they talk, what they read, and what experiences they have already had before coming to school (Goodman 1986).

Getting Your Feet Wet

Becoming a "whole language teacher" begins from within. First, a teacher must have a desire to change. Among those who have begun to move toward a whole language approach, a consistent attitude seems to prevail: my teaching and my classroom can be better. Yet for those attracted to a holistic rather than a reductionist philosophy, there is also uncertainty: "This sounds great, but how do I get there?" The journey may seem risky because a whole language curriculum does not consist of five, six, or seven basic procedures. Some teachers begin very tentatively, with a "let me test the water" attitude, and in different places, some with a change in their approach to reading, others with writing. Still others like the notion of a thematic approach. But these personal journeys toward change are best reported by the teachers themselves.

REFLECTIONS OF THOSE WHO HAVE TESTED THE WATER

Margaret Glass

Margaret Glass is an experienced whole language teacher and often serves as a consultant in neighboring school districts. She began integrating a whole language philosophy into her curriculum when she was a teacher of primary-aged children who were identified as mentally retarded or learning disabled. One day, while I talked with Margaret about her classroom, she reflected back on her first experiences with whole language and on how much she had learned by observing the children and following where they led.

I started in whole language using Big Books, then themes. I also wanted to have centers because kids need time to explore and experiment. When there is a set schedule and set lesson plans, there is no free choice for the children. When children go to the various centers, this is the best time for me. I can see what they are doing, what they have created, what they have done with the center idea. This is when I do my best kidwatching. I get to observe how they are thinking. It's interesting that at the end of the center time they always end up in groups. They share with one another, ask each other for help, listen to tapes together. Sometimes a few like to be alone, but most of the time they want to be together.

In the beginning I didn't allow my students to write on their own. They copied my writing. Now I understand that writing is a developmental process, and the children learn it the same way they learn oral language. They don't need to be directly taught. They might make an *e* backwards, but the next day they will turn it around and finally get it right. I've observed a pattern when young children are first learning to write. First, there is scribbling, then symbol-like scribbles with a letter, then all letters, and they will fill the page with letters, they will copy off of charts, copy book pages, copy sentences and whole books. Finally, they begin invented spelling.

Also in the beginning, I didn't give them enough time to write. Their writing didn't develop as much as their reading. Now I give them more writing time. They can choose to write during their free time, and we have a more formal writing time. We write a lot of group stories based on books we have read or information we have learned. I observe a lot of generalizations that the children make. We have a pet hamster, and when I brought the hamster to class there was a lot of interest by the students, so we did a unit on hamsters . . . They observed the hamster, recorded observations, and did library research. We decided to do a fun story about the hamster. It was incredible. The students took the information they had learned about hamsters and included it in their fictional story. They also used a style from one of their favorite books, which uses a lot of phrases like "under the bridge," "over the stream." So in their story they incorporated these same kinds of phrases.

Another good illustration of the generalizations they are able to make was when I read them a little book about Martin Luther King in January. The children then dictated the following sentences: "Martin Luther King told the people that black and white people should sit together, eat together, and play together. He was real, real smart." Then in February we talked about Abraham Lincoln and how he freed the slaves. The kids pointed out that Abraham Lincoln was like Martin Luther King—they had made that connection on their own!

Margaret said she usually tries to have a general plan for what her students will be doing, but many times they take her in a different direction. She has learned to "go with their flow" and takes her cues from them. Over and over, Margaret noted how suprised she was that they could do so well, that they had progressed so much. She believes that with a label come lower expectations. She has discovered that her students can learn and will learn when given meaningful opportunities.

Ann McLaughlin

Ann McLaughlin was a student in one of my graduate classes on the literacy development of students with mild to moderate learning problems. The majority of the class were teachers who had been teaching from zero to fifteen years. It was a dynamic group that actively interacted and shared ideas. The teachers were at different stages in their experimentation with a more holistic approach to teaching. At the time, Ann taught students in intermediate grades who were identified as learning disabled. She wrote the following paper:

Each year my school district holds a Young Authors Celebration in which students are encouraged to write and illustrate their own books. The students may create their books at home or at school, may write about any subject and may complete their finished product by handwriting, typewriting or computer printing. Of the entries submitted in each school a committee of teachers chooses fifteen books to be presented at the high school on Young Authors Day.

Each year I have indifferently watched as this celebration came and went without much thought of my students participating. After all, I thought, what in the world would my students with learning disabilities write about? How would I ever get all of my students motivated and find the time to help them make corrections and revisions of their work? How would their writing compare to other students their age? And, most importantly, what would the committee of my peers think of my abilities as a teacher once they read what my students produced? Young Authors would definitely be a risky venture for my class, but this year I began to have a change of heart.

I have always tried to be an advocate for my students and to prove how "normal" they are to everyone in my building, yet with something so simple as writing a story I wouldn't even encourage them to try. Finally, I was beginning to see the light. Special education students are already excluded from so many activities at our school, why was I holding them back? Why not cautiously take a chance on Young Authors and see what they could do?

So, I introduced the idea to my students and "they were off!" Pencils flying furiously, they wrote about everything from "The Halloween Parade" to "Bart Simpson in the Ghetto." We spent about thirty minutes each day writing, drawing, coloring and revising the books. The student response was so enthusiastic that other students with learning disabilities who were not in my homeroom asked if they could join my class during this time each day to write their own books. The results of this "cautious venture" were far better than I could have imagined.

Of the eighty-eight students who submitted books in our building, only fifteen would be chosen to represent our school, and guess what? Miracle of miracles one of my fifth-graders made it into this elite group. She had written a story entitled, "The Crying Rose." It wasn't perfect but it was good enough to be noticed by our committee. The recognition for the other students who participated was also much more than I expected. Each student was treated to a "party" at which there was a storyteller and Young Authors buttons and cake. The kids thought this was great, but there was still more. The Young Authors had a group picture taken for our yearbook and they each received a certificate at the awards ceremony on the last day of school. What a tremendous boost to their egos!

We will definitely try Young Authors again next year. The tangible rewards along with the psychological rewards far outweigh any doubts I had about letting my students take a chance. My message to other teachers of students with learning disabilities is, "Be a cautious risk-taker. Give your kids every opportunity for success and always let everyone know that kids with learning disabilities are *normal* kids first and foremost."

Teresa Townsend

Teresa Townsend was interested in change, and the whole language philosophy appealed to her intuitive sense of the direction she should take. As part of her master's degree program she had to fulfill a field study requirement that she conduct research or develop and implement a curriculum change. This was the gentle push that she needed. She decided to introduce a whole language approach in her resource room for elementary students with learning disabilities:

> My reason was twofold. First, on a personal level, I liked the humanistic approach of whole language in which kids are respected and trusted. I like the holistic aspect in which reading, language, and spelling could all be tied in together. The second reason was based on the great difficulty my students have with reading and writing. Some dislike reading and many are bored with the basals and worksheets. I wanted my students to enjoy reading and discover the joy of well-written books and literature.

Teresa began her project by reading and learning as much as she could about whole language. Her discoveries confirmed that this was the approach she wanted to try.

> I discovered that whole language is a theory, and that it does not rely on any particular type of material or method. It requires respect for and trust of the learner, and the classroom is a community where interaction between students and the teacher is valued. Students come into the classroom with a certain amount of knowledge they can share and build upon. Mutual trust combined with student ownership of classroom activities helps the students become active learners. Another important aspect of whole language is the blending of curriculum—not keeping reading, spelling, and written language as separate entities. Also, the teacher is a facilitator. "Leading from behind" is an important concept.

After she had done a great deal of reading, Teresa observed a whole language classroom. Next, she established personal goals for her students. The main goal was to expand her reading program from basals to books, stories, and literature sets. She also wanted to combine her reading and writing programs. Previously her students had read two to four pages a day from the basal, learned vocabulary word lists, completed comprehension sheets from reading workbooks, and occasionally read together from a "free time" book. Writing consisted of "edit" sentences (with no punctuation), sentences comprising spelling words, and creative writing on Friday. Teresa considered the changes she should make.

> Where to start and how much to change? I started by putting less emphasis on the basal readers. The basals have some disadvantages. Basals mark a student's reading level, or lack of it. Nothing is worse than to have a third- or

fourth-grade student in a first-grade basal reader. It is demeaning socially, and the stories at that point are not interesting or age appropriate. Many of my poorest readers have been through the same reader more than one time. Motivation and interest? It fades quickly. On the plus side, basal readers do have a good selection of reading material on the appropriate grade level. Therefore, I decided that I would not rule out using the basal, but it would not be my primary reading method or material. I chose to use literature sets from the library and books of my own. In addition to group activities I decided to attend to individual IEP reading goals by providing time for each child to read to me individually from books that the students chose. I incorporated writing with journal time and writing activities based on the stories and books they were reading or current events or topics of interest.

At first Teresa was worried that she would not have enough materials and creative ideas. She anticipated that the students would exhibit their typical "I don't care" attitude. But her fears quickly evaporated as her students took the lead in generating ideas and topics to explore. She was also concerned about assessment. Her school district has a minimum basic skills list that students are expected to master for each grade level. Her special students are required to meet a certain percentage or show improvement from a baseline sample on IEP goals.

How could I incorporate my holistic program and yet meet the demands of the school's curriculum? I decided to set aside a specific time to devote to teaching those skills. At first I allocated two thirty-minute sessions per week for skills instruction. In reality the time format varied. With some groups I used the arbitrary thirty-minute skills lesson, but then I began to look for ways to incorporate a "holistic" approach to teaching the skills. I was not always successful, but each time that I was, I felt great. For example, the basal includes library, encyclopedia, and dictionary skills. These were quite easy to incorporate into our study of current event topics. I taught main idea and summarizing as we discussed reading selections. I would ask such questions as, "What do you think the main idea is? Can you summarize this story for me?" I used the words "main idea" and "summarize" so that they would be familiar with the concepts and terms when they took their reading tests.

The results of the assessment were encouraging. My fifth graders tested out on grade level in reading for the first time. They would start "on level" next year! My fourth-grade students did not do quite as well. One student made an F in reading in his mainstream class. However, his language and science grades came up from F to a D and C. My third graders really shined—three made the honor roll. They were the most open to my new way of doing things, and they loved it. All of them passed reading, with the exception of one girl who moved here in April.

This year was a pleasure to teach and as the end of the year neared, I found that I was not counting days as many of my colleagues were. I will admit that I look forward to having time off this summer, but the drudgery and tedious feeling of repetition that plagues me annually in April and May was not present this year. I also discovered that I enjoyed my students more. I did not view my students as behavior problems and "lazy" learners. In April and May, particularly after spring break, it is difficult to interest students in academic tasks. This year, with the "holistic" approach, it was not a problem.

I will admit that all was not perfect, and I have many areas that need improvement. I will continue to change and gradually incorporate a more holistic curriculum. All in all, I learned a great deal from this project. I have much more to learn, but I have accomplished the greatest tasks of all—getting started and taking a risk.

Rachael Hobbs

Like Teresa, Rachael Hobbs also received a gentle push. She began her research as a result of an assignment in a course she was taking for her master's program. As a resource teacher for junior high and high school students, Rachael was concerned about whether strategy instruction was compatible with a whole language approach. She used Ken Goodman's book, *What's Whole in Whole Language* (1986), to confirm that it was possible. Goodman believes that "expression (writing) and comprehension (reading) strategies are built during functional, meaningful, relevant language use" (p. 39). He advises teachers to "begin developing strategy lessons for your least effective readers. Suitable strategy lessons will help them build the basic strategies of prediction, inference, self-monitoring, and self-correction" (p. 72).

A couple of years after Rachael began to use a more holistic teaching approach, I interviewed her about her initial involvement.

Charlotte: What was your teaching schedule and routine before you began moving toward whole language?

Rachael: My class is a resource room and most of my kids came to me for 49 percent of the day. It was not unusual to have ten to fifteen kids at one time. Sometimes I would be teaching three or four subjects at one time . . . English, math, history. In addition, other kids not scheduled in at that time were allowed to come down and take tests.

Charlotte: When you started moving in the direction of whole language, what things did you begin to change?

Rachael: I started looking at the curriculum and what they were supposed to be learning . . . concepts that I thought they needed. I looked at alternative ways to acquire these skills and concepts through reading literature . . . We read the novel, *Where the Red Fern Grows.*

Rachel selected *Where the Red Fern Grows* by using informal reading inventories to determine interest and reading level. She also referred to lists of recommended books for various reading ages. From the information she gathered, she chose four books. She gave the students a brief synopsis of each book as well as the opportunity to look through each book. They chose *Where The Red Fern Grows.*

Charlotte: How did you handle the reading of the novel? Did you read aloud to them? Did they read along with their own copies?

Rachael: Yes, I got copies for each one and they read along. One of the problems I was working with was fluency and comprehension. This was something that was lacking in their background. They hadn't been read aloud to a lot, and so we needed to start at the ground level and work up . . . One of the reasons I read out loud was so that I could stop: "At this word I saw a funny look on some of your faces. Do you understand what that word means. What could you do to find out? Let's read on to see if it tells us more." Or I would stop because I knew where the book was going. If I knew something was coming up, or there had been some foreshadowing, I would ask them to write a prediction.

Charlotte: What kinds of activities did you do?

Rachael: We did mapping. They made a scale model of what the farm would look like. They wrote stories about a favorite pet, and some wrote about pets that had died. We wrote a lot of [chapter] summaries . . . they did them together. They would sit down and talk, "Well, I remember this part . . . I remember this other part," and then they would put all their ideas together.

Charlotte: You didn't have to get any special materials other than your books?

Rachael: No.

Charlotte: Did you continue using your workbooks?

Rachael: No, we quit using basal readers and workbooks.

Charlotte: What were the kids' reactions to that change?

Rachael: They liked not having to do the workbooks; they abhorred them anyway. They were real excited; they liked the books . . . At first they didn't like to write—they had a lot more writing than they were used to and that didn't go over real well with them. They eventually got over it because I let them work cooperatively on writing, and it wasn't nearly as bad as [writing] individually.

Charlotte: Did you give them some guidance?

Rachael: Sometimes . . . at first I really directed where I wanted them to go. Then I moved back and let them take the initiative. But they needed to have the guidance to see what the thinking processes were . . . I used a lot of mapping. So that's the format they picked up. I didn't have a sheet or anything they used, but they picked it up and used that [strategy] on their own. To this day I still see them using maps.

Charlotte: What effects did you see? You started at midyear, right?

Rachael: Tremendous! Because we mainstreamed every one of those kids at the end of that year.

Charlotte: So they went from 49 percent of the day in your class to what?

Rachael: They would come in during their study hall—maybe one hour a day.

Charlotte: They had been in your class . . .

Rachael: Three to four hours a day.

Charlotte: Were they successful? No problems?

Rachael: Yes, they maintained B's and C's in their [general education] classroom for the most part. There were a few in the D range but none failed.

Charlotte: That first year when you started, what advantage did you see? In other words, you had a real comparison to what you had been doing, a programmed approach compared to a more holistic approach.

Rachael: The biggest advantage—I saw them start to have fun in class. They enjoyed it. It wasn't, "Oh no, do we have to do this?" as they came staggering down the stairs. They would want to be there. It's not unusual, not only for the kids assigned to my room, but also "regular" kids that go by my door or in study hall, to pop in and sit down while I'm having a discussion. Another big thing is that they started taking active control of their own life. They knew what they wanted to get out of something.

Charlotte: What disadvantages did you see?

Rachael: I don't know if it's a disadvantage. My own self doubt . . . if I was covering all that we needed to be covering . . . but they were able to be successful.

Charlotte: Did you miss the structure you had before?

Rachael: Yes. It's hard as a teacher who's trying to be that person in front of the class teaching, controlling everything, to turn loose that control. There are days I look around and think, "Is this chaos or are they actually learning something from all this?" It is hard not to step in and put control back on top when things get out of hand or a little wild. They have to learn the process, too. At first it's like total freedom for them . . . they tend to try to take advantage of it, but when they see they are held accountable and responsible . . ., they start putting controls on themselves.

HOW WAS THE WATER?

Each teacher who described and discussed her initial experiments with whole language started from a different place, but they all seemed to have similar reactions. Their starting points reflected their existing curriculum, the ages of their students, and the type of special education classroom they had, as well as their students' needs and their own personal goals. They all wanted to help students to cope and succeed outside of the safe environment of their special classroom. They all talked about the joy of learning and teaching. For all of them, teaching became a process of relinquishing control and taking cues from the students themselves. They were not disappointed. The water was great.

Creating a Child-Centered Environment

As a university professor, I work with both inservice and preservice teachers. Preservice teachers, students in my university classroom who are on the eve of graduation, often experience PRJ (Pre-Reality Jitters). Slowly they come to the realization that in the not-too-distant future they may actually have to face a classroom of children or young people for whom they are responsible. Being a teacher will no longer be a simple matter of going to class, reading, and discussing the pros and cons of theory, discipline, classroom management, and other issues. They begin projecting themselves into the situation where they will actually have to *do it*. This is the time when the jitters really start, so, it's not unusual to hear them implore, "Please, just tell me what I'm supposed to do, how, when, how many times, how long."

Inservice teachers who are interested in introducing whole language theory into their teaching may experience some of this same nervousness. While they are not so panic-stricken, they do appreciate concrete information on how to get started. The first move is the toughest in any new endeavor, whether it's going on a diet, beginning an exercise program, auditioning for a play, or skydiving. Once we get started, the rest of the journey doesn't seem so scary.

Chapter 3 highlighted the experiences of teachers beginning their journey into whole language teaching. All of them developed a plan about how they would begin. This chapter offers some suggestions about how to take the plunge into whole language and develop an initial plan. Most people like to begin new endeavors with simple, concrete actions. I suggest creating a literacy environment (see Figure 4.1).

LANGUAGE- AND PRINT-RICH CLASSROOMS

By analyzing emergent literacy theory and their own classroom experience and observation, Nancy Taylor, Irene Blum, and David Logsdon (1986) identified the characteristics of language- and print-rich classrooms, and their findings are useful in assessing the status of language and print in an individual classroom. These characteristics include multiple and varied stimuli for reading

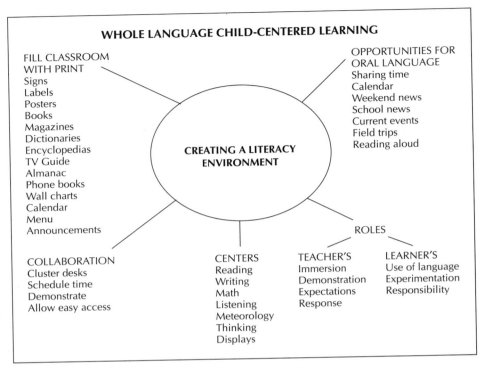

FIGURE 4.1   Whole language child-centered learning

and writing, such as trade books, wall charts, and information books; accessible and functional displays of children's language products; the integration of written language throughout the curriculum and of print throughout daily routines, such as attendance and lunch count, and activities that focus on children's interests and needs.

Environmental Print

The classroom should display a wide variety of print. For very young learners, or learners who are having difficulty with print, it is helpful to label common objects, such as *wall, door, desk, pencil sharpener, file cabinet, window, blinds, shades.* Some would argue that labeling objects in the classroom environment is not appropriate because there are no labels in the "real" environment outside the classroom. I have observed, however, that if the labels are used as active texts, they can help children make the connection between oral and written language. Labels become active texts, for example, when children identify what should be labeled and when teachers point to the labels and offer students the opportunity to refer to them. The labels become an environmental dictionary: when children are ready to incorporate these words into their writing, they know where to find them. Eventually the labels themselves become unnecessary.

Other kinds of environmental print can include informational wall charts and frequently read songs, rhymes, or short stories, which can be copied on chart paper and hung in a prominent, easy-to-see location. Other information can be displayed in the same way—the calendar, lunch menus, posters, schedules, important announcements, information about holidays, and classroom rules.

In a whole language classroom student work is itself a major resource. Students' writing and artwork quickly fill the bulletin boards and wall space. To create more hanging space, some teachers string wire from one side of the room to the other. Many display student-authored books, which are read and reread by students and visitors.

Learners like to feel ownership of the environment in which they spend so much time. Jean Meuth, a special education teacher, came up with an analogy for her special education students—classroom: home: castle. Because they spent a great deal of time in the classroom, it was much like their home, and they should treat their home as if it were a castle. She inspired her students to have some pride in their classroom and in their school. They decided that while their classroom looked very nice, the hallways were dreary and boring, and that posters and artwork might liven things up. Jean's students not only received permission from the principal, but they also made a presentation to their school board requesting a little money to purchase items for their project. To their delight, the board supported their idea.

The invitation to think about their environment led students to a comprehensive and memorable learning activity. Jean admitted that she never dreamed her students could accomplish so much and that making a presentation to the board of education to solicit funds was not an objective that she had anticipated. But given the opportunity and their teacher's encouragement, her students took some responsibility for their learning environment and achieved a meaningful result.

Social Learning Environment

In traditional classrooms, the desks are arranged in rows. In some special education classrooms desks are placed around the walls or study carrels ("offices") facing the wall. These arrangements may serve a purpose, but they do little to encourage student cooperation, collaboration, or communication. In fact, these arrangements were probably designed to discourage just such "friendly" interaction.

Whole language classrooms encourage oral language development in a community of learners; students need to be able to learn together and support each other. Talking to one another doesn't necessarily mean students have been diverted "off task." They learn from each other when they discuss and share ideas.

The way desks and tables are arranged should communicate the message that it is okay to work together. A simple arrangement, such as clustering desks or tables together in the center of the room, promotes a communicative atmosphere and clears space for setting up learning centers in various corners or nooks. Tables where several students can work at the same time also encourages them to talk as they learn.

Not all children know how to—or choose to—work cooperatively; some may find the close proximity of other students distracting. One solution is to create an alternative place, such as a small partitioned area, where these students can work on their own some of the time. At the same time, cooperative work is expected in our society. Students will not learn appropriate work and social skills if we do not demonstrate these skills and give students a chance to practice them (see Chapter 6 for ideas on developing group skills).

Oral Language Environment

Special education students are sometimes less adept at oral language than their nondisabled peers. A simple, powerful way to enhance their oral language skills is to create an environment where they can listen and express themselves without fear of making mistakes or of being ridiculed or interrupted. Students feel valued when we show an interest in what they say, especially if we invite them to share their feelings and ideas. If we avoid judgmental remarks and listen with sincere warmth and respect, we encourage students to experiment with language and to become more proficient in using language as a tool for thinking and learning.

A sharing time during the first hour of the morning or at the beginning of a particular class period provides a context for speaking and listening. A variety of formats are possible—a set time each day, or if students have different schedules every day, perhaps one day a week. Students' contributions can be recorded on the chalkboard or on chart paper. Teachers of young or more delayed children find this a good time to discuss the calendar and the weather.

Sometimes students with learning or behavior difficulties find it hard to draw on what they already know and may not know what to talk about. Teachers can encourage talk by throwing out some possible topics:

- *Weekend news:* What students did over the previous weekend.
- *The week that was:* A recap of the entire week's (class or school) events.
- *In the News:* Reports about local, state, or national news.
- *Did you hear the one about . . .:* Students prepare a joke, a riddle, or an interesting story in advance to share with the class. (Demonstrate and discuss what would and would not be appropriate beforehand.)
- *Roots:* Students compile an oral history of their family. (Again, a demonstration or mini-lesson is in order; model the kinds of questions students might ask their parents, grandparents, or aunts and uncles; brainstorm with the class about what they would like to find out.)
- *Trips and other experiences:* Enrich students' background experiences by taking trips and organizing other shared experiences, such as cooking together. Students can not only talk about the experience afterwards, they can also write about it and read what they have written.
- *Guest speakers:* Students prepare questions in advance when guests visit and act as tour guides to displays and projects in progress.

It's fun for students to keep written accounts of "The Week That Was" and compile them into individual autobiographies or a class book, always a class favorite. My junior high class of students with hearing impairments made a Big Book: together each week we created a language experience story, based on the week's events, which we later transferred to poster board, and added to our book. We also took pictures of many of our class activities, and the photographs became the illustrations. Our class-made book presented the ongoing saga of the year's events. We displayed the book on an easel, and it was not unusual to find not only "special" students but "nonspecial" kids reading and rereading it.

Along with more traditional kinds of shared experience, discussion and demonstration of the kinds of language we use can be helpful: for example, the ways in which book language is different from conversational language or the differences between playground language, home language, church language, and classroom language. These demonstrations are especially useful for children who have difficulty in adapting their language to a particular audience or situation.

Stephanie Jacob, a teacher of ten- to twelve-year-olds whose reported IQs range from 35 to 69, helped her students learn how to conduct an interview. Each week she designates one student as "Star of the Week." On Monday the "Star" stands in front of the class while the other students ask questions about favorite foods, colors, TV shows, and so on. As the students interview the "Star," Stephanie models notetaking by writing key phrases to summarize the "Star's" answers on a large piece of paper. When the interview is finished, Stephanie posts the notes on the chalkboard, and students use them as an aid in writing a story about the "Star." When I visited the class, I was deemed the "Visitor" of the week. The students followed a similar procedure, and I was quite impressed with the questions they asked and the illustrated stories they wrote (see Figure 4.2).

Reading aloud to children is another way to demonstrate language. Through literature children can experience a variety of language uses—conversation, persuasion, exposition, and interpretation. They can also identify with the characters in the stories. Literature has been used as an intervention technique for individuals with mental retardation, children with emotional problems, children with behavioral disorders, children with learning disabilities, children who have been abused, children from dysfunctional families, and adolescents at-risk. Literature emphasizing some of the themes children encounter in their own lives improves their self-perception and helps them with their own circumstances (Gerber and Harris 1983; Miller 1993; Randolph and Gredler 1985). (See the thematic list of children's books at the end of the book.)

Building learners' confidence so they dare to risk expressing themselves orally and to ask pertinent questions, and helping learners listen lead naturally to increased adeptness with written language. Once learners have expressed their thoughts orally, they have a solid place from which to explore written language. Learning to listen and ask questions shows students that a reader is much like a listener, and an author much like a speaker.

Learning/Activity Centers

Many teachers have discovered that learning centers in the classroom can serve as learning tools and as a way to organize activities during a time of potential disorder. Michelle Clark's students (K–6) arrived at different times during the first hour or so of the morning. The variable schedule was the result of bus schedules and general education classes in which her students were included. It was difficult for her to set aside large spaces for centers because of the small

FIGURE 4.2   Patrick's story about the "visitor" of the week

size of her classroom and the number of students. She did, however, have bookshelves filled with books, a small table with writing materials, and a shelf with headphones and a tape recorder. When students entered the room, they could choose to read, write, or go to the listening station. Michelle found that these informal centers were an ideal way to organize the students' daily comings and goings with little confusion. While students were engaged in their self-chosen literacy activity, she was able to do the required morning paperwork (attendance, lunch count, and so on). Morning routines like these provide the structure and organization special learners often need. Unlike the traditional folder system, with assigned worksheets, learning centers and work stations allow students to choose what they will do and promote decision-making.

Learning and activity centers also foster individualization and oral language development. As I visit whole language classrooms for special learners, I have observed how creative and functional they can be. Many of these classrooms are multiage. One of my favorite scenes is that of an older student and a younger student huddled in a corner reading together. Usually the older student is reading aloud to the younger student, although it is not unusual for a younger student to practice reading with someone older. The center time seems to encourage a natural cooperation and support among students like that in classrooms of children with diverse abilities. Children feel free to support each other because the centers erase the barriers of standardized curriculum.

If room is available, a reading corner with a bit of carpet lets students sit close together while they share a book or while you read aloud. Rachael Hobbs used about one-third of her junior high-high school resource room for the reading corner/library. The three sofas and small teacher's desk create a living-room/den atmosphere. During free reading time, students have permission to "get comfortable" (some choose to stretch out) as if they were at home. Rachael also takes advantage of the same relaxed atmosphere when she is reading aloud or conducting mini-lessons.

Barb Kinsella, who teaches first graders with communication disorders, also creates a "homey" atmosphere in her classroom. An old-fashioned rocker sits in one corner with lots of books close at hand. During read-aloud time, the children gather around Barb on the carpeted floor and listen intently as she reads a favorite story for the tenth or eleventh time, or sometimes a new one.

Along with the reading corner there is, of course, the class library. The library should include books on many different topics at many different reading levels and include fiction, nonfiction, reference books, magazines, newspapers, and TV schedules. Some teachers like to spotlight authors and display new or special books.

A listening center with tape recorders, cassettes, and headphones allows students to listen to recorded books and music. I often observe students wearing headphones intently listening and following along in a book. What books do they listen to? Usually books that have been previously introduced to the whole class. The listening station provides an invaluable opportunity for students with reading difficulties to get further exposure to a good reading model.

Margaret Glass created a writing center in her classroom with stacks of paper of different colors and sizes as well as colored pencils, crayons, felt markers, and pens. Her students love to experiment. One day James carefully lined up markers of different colors—red, blue, orange, green, and purple. Then he began writing a list of words, each in a different color. I asked him what he was writing. Without looking at me, he answered in a voice filled with pride, "These are words I know how to spell!"

Sitting next to James was Tisha. She had chosen to copy a page from a book she was reading. As she finished writing each line, she read it aloud. Tisha had not yet reached the writing stage James had. She was just learning how to spell words and had chosen, quite independently, to use a familiar book as her guide. Still another child was writing a book of his own about dinosaurs based on all the information he had learned in a thematic unit. An incredible amount of individualized learning was going on all around the room. Students were working and learning at their own levels without worksheets. Where was the teacher? She was sitting with a student and listening as he read his "homework" book. At the end of the day the students select a book for each student to read at home. The book goes into a plastic bag and then into the student's home-work folder. At the beginning of the year Margaret talks with parents about how to use the homework book (see Chapter 14).

Margaret engages in "kid watching" throughout the day, but she uses individual reading time to focus on particular children. "Kid watching" is a term coined by Yetta Goodman (1985) to describe the observation of learners reacting to print in a variety of social and cultural settings—on the playground, in the hallway, during sustained silent reading, during writing time, during oral reading, and so on. When Margaret listens to her students read individually, she focuses on their ability to use strategies such as prediction, their fluency, and how much assistance they need, noting her observations in a spiral notebook. She adds more notes during her observations of students' perform-ance in small group settings, writing time, and whole class discussions. Later, she will reread her notes and assess her students' progress.

Besides writing in personal journals, writing words, and writing books, students also like to write notes and messages. A class post office made from a refrigerator box, or personal mailboxes placed on a shelf near the writing center, encourage this natural use of written language.

Centers also work well with thematic studies. Stephanie Jacob organizes classroom centers around ongoing theme studies. During their study of color, for example, she set up a variety of activities. Students could mix primary colors with food coloring, make rainbow toast, chart the different colors of candy scooped from a big bowl, and look through a kaleidoscope to create their own color pattern. First, she explained the activity at each center; then students went to the center of their choice. When they had completed an activity, they rotated to another center. It was interesting to note that Stephanie did not have to direct their activity. Through her demonstrations and their experience of the center format throughout the year, the children had become familiar with the routine, and even somewhat independent, and were able to take responsibility for completing each activity.

A "thinking station" is another intriguing place for students to stop for a while. The teacher can supply puzzles and brain teasers for the thinking station, or it can simply be a place where students can get together to talk over a plan, a project, or a problem. It's also okay if a student goes there alone to think. If it seems that students might take advantage of the situation, it is still worth trying and then making adaptations accordingly. In my classroom I found that students used the thinking table after they had finished a project or an assignment; they might work alone on a puzzle, browse through encyclopedias, or work together. It was not at all unusual for someone who was still working to solicit help from a student at the thinking table.

An art center can also serve as a nucleus for self-expression. Special-edu-cation teacher Pam Evans's room often includes a painting center with easels, paper, and tempera paints. Students may express themselves with the paints in any way they choose (she also provides old shirts to wear over clothes). Because the painting area can only handle two students at a time, she has installed a sign-up sheet. The only rule is that students have to be considerate and allow other students on the sign-up sheet time to paint.

Learners of all ages enjoy displays and exhibits of just about anything: shells, rocks, fossils, old bones, art prints, or a personal special collection. A class pet such as a hamster, a turtle, or fish, can also enhance the learning environment. Students not only learn about how to take care of an animal, they also have a wonderful opportunity to observe, chart information, and write. Margaret Glass's classroom houses several pets that stimulate curiosity and learning. When a hamster was brought to class, for example, the students learned to feed and care for it and were responsible for doing so. Their interest in the hamster led to a broader study of mammals. During one of my visits, students took turns sharing interesting facts about hamsters, and mammals in general, and explained to me why a hamster is classified as a mammal. They learned all of this information not because it was part of a prescribed curriculum but because of their natural curiosity. Margaret provided a stimulus and then allowed them to be curious and search for answers.

Learning centers individualized for "on level" practice do not necessarily comply with the whole language philosophy, whereas centers established for discovery, exploration, and constructive knowledge complement the notion of child-centered learning. They provide children with an organized format for exploration and discovery and teachers with an excellent opportunity for kid watching. Children naturally individualize their learning by choosing activities on their own "level." The teacher does not dictate what will happen: the learning occurs naturally. And centers help to create a relaxed atmosphere, which sends children the message that learning can be a pleasant endeavor.

IN CLOSING

It is possible to extend the whole language philosophy to the instruction of *special* learners. The learners I have mentioned in this chapter are all identified with various disabilities, but I have intentionally refrained from referring to them so that children's learning could be the primary focus.

How then should we begin to facilitate learning for "special" learners? Regardless of their placement—in a general education class or a special class—a good place to begin is the classroom itself. Meaningful print displayed all over the room, a classroom environment that allows learners to learn from each other, and constructive opportunities to continue to develop oral language skills are all worthwhile goals. In addition, learning and activity centers set aside a designated space where students can explore reading, writing, art, math, or whatever they find interesting. At the same time, centers provide an organized way for students to engage in child-centered learning rather than teacher-centered activities.

The Teacher's Role

Creating a whole language classroom environment is part of the larger process of immersion. "Immersion" is the recognition that when children are beginning to learn oral language, they are exposed to thousands of demonstrations from birth. They are immersed in language in whole and meaningful contexts. Similarly, learners who are just beginning to understand written language, or are having difficulty with the processes of reading and writing, should be immersed in whole, functional, meaningful written language.

A physical classroom environment that encourages immersion is not enough. Appropriate teacher attitudes and actions are an essential contribution to the *whole* learning environment.

Brian Cambourne (1988) has developed a model illustrating the conditions necessary for literacy learning. His model is based on his observation of the optimal conditions for learning oral language. Immersion is at the top because it filters into everything that happens. The foundation of the model is engagement. It incorporates reciprocity between teacher and learner: both are active participants. This chapter will focus on the teacher's role.

IMMERSION

It is not enough to immerse learners in environmental print; they also need to interact with written language in as many different ways as possible. Teachers who work with beginning or less able readers might turn to familiar product logos (Coca-Cola, McDonald's, Ford, and Hershey for example) to emphasize the message, *"You are a reader."* Even students who have been labeled "nonreaders" can recognize these logos. Children might make a game of collecting samples from newspapers and magazines and gather them together into a class *Logo Book* for reading and rereading. Recognizing these logos *is* reading, and teachers should stress this fact. The act of reading becomes an attainable goal—especially for those who have been told that they can't read.

To enable students to develop their literacy skills and build confidence, the teacher should read aloud highly predictable stories that feature repetition. Teachers of young children like to use Big Books, which have predictable phrases or rhymes, so everyone in the class can see them. The teacher reads the text while the students follow along in what becomes a *shared reading* experience. Because the stories have repeated phrases and rhymes the children can soon read the text along with the teacher, and in no time they can read the book without assistance. This technique works well with charts and rhymes displayed on a wall or on a bulletin board.

The shared reading experience is an excellent way to give students confidence in reading, but it does not have to be limited exclusively to young children. Older children who are having difficulty with reading also benefit from predictable stories. These older learners frequently have little confidence in their ability to read and attempt to decode words letter-by-letter, so that they lose any sense of a meaningful story. Unfortunately, Big Books and predictable stories are often geared toward young children, and older students, who can benefit from them, may be turned off. To avoid this problem, I have introduced poems and song lyrics, which provide predictability and repetition and work at a variety of age levels. One poem I have used with great success with children of different ages is Mother Goose's *"Poor Old Lady"*:

> Poor old lady, she swallowed a fly.
> I don't know why she swallowed a fly.
> Poor old lady I think she'll die.
>
> Poor old lady, she swallowed a spider.
> It squirmed and wriggled and turned inside her.
> She swallowed the spider to catch the fly.
> I don't know why she swallowed a fly.
> Poor old lady, I think she'll die.
>
> Poor old lady, she swallowed a bird.
> How absurd! She swallowed a bird.
> She swallowed the bird to catch the spider.
> She swallowed the spider to catch the fly.
> I don't know why she swallowed a fly.
> Poor old lady, I think she'll die.
>
> Poor old lady, she swallowed a cat.
> Think of that! She swallowed a cat.
> She swallowed the cat to catch the bird.
> She swallowed the bird to catch the spider.
> She swallowed the spider to catch the fly.
> Poor old lady, I think she'll die.

Because of its silly events, older readers have particular fun with this poem. Students also enjoy doing illustrations or writing their own version.

As Bobbi Fisher (1991) points out, shared reading creates a noncompetitive atmosphere; students participate at their own developmental level. They are allowed to approximate and self-correct and make sense for themselves as they work toward becoming independent, self-regulating readers.

Teachers have a primary responsibility to immerse their students in visual print and in interactions with written language. The immersion process is intended to recreate with written language the kind of immersion in oral language an individual experiences from birth. The teacher plays the role of classroom expert and coordinator. She creates a print-filled, language-rich environment that allows students to take control of their own learning.

DEMONSTRATION

It is practically impossible for teachers to immerse students in language without demonstrating language. In a whole language classroom, reading and writing are valued as meaningful, and when students read and write stories, teachers have an opportunity to demonstrate how they approach and solve problems when they write. They can model thinking aloud, which gives learners not only the "how" but also the "why" of what they are doing.

Teachers who feel a little unsure about how to begin a whole language class often find that *reading aloud* is a solid basis for a meaningful demonstration. According to Jim Trelease (1989), reading aloud converts negative attitudes about reading into positive attitudes. It is especially beneficial to students who tend to read in a halting or labored fashion and to concentrate on "sounding out" words. When teachers or parents read for pleasure, the chances that their listeners will engage in the same kind of behavior increase.

I understood the power of reading aloud in working with one student after school. Among other problems, Stephen read with poor fluency and almost no expression. As part of our routine I began to read aloud with lots of enthusiasm and intonation and encouraged him to join me. For "homework," I asked him to practice by himself. One day his mother reported that Stephen had been practicing. "At first," she said, "I couldn't imagine what he was doing. His voice sounded strange. Then when I went upstairs and listened to him more closely, I realized that he was mimicking your accent." (I grew up in Texas, and to people in the Midwest I have an accent). I asked, "How is his expression?" "Oh," she said, "his expression is great!"

A positive reading model, Jim Trelease adds, also allows learners to gain new information and expose them to the pleasures of reading, rich vocabulary, good sentence and story structure, and often a book they might not otherwise read themselves. It stimulates their imagination, stretches their attention span, improves listening comprehension, nurtures emotional development, and establishes a reading and writing connection. "Is there a textbook or workbook," Trelease asks, "that will accomplish all this in a fifteen-minute period?"

Reading aloud teaches children so much about reading—how to hold a book, turn pages, and direct their eyes from left to right; how to look for story clues in illustrations, predict and retell story events. Most important, children learn that the print on the page means words, and that this written code makes sense. Teachers notice that students whose reading is choppy begin to read more fluently—in phrases rather than word by word—and with more expression and meaning. Reading aloud enriches children's vocabulary and spurs discussion. And it serves as a relaxing break that gives them time to wind down.

When I observe teachers reading aloud to their students, I am always drawn to the same thing: students interaction with the text. With young children it is not unusual for at least one or two to step in front of the book (which the teacher is holding so everyone can see) and point out something of particular interest in one of the pictures. While older children may not be so "rude," they may blurt out what they think will happen or offer a personal comment about a particular character. These interactions interest me because they show that these children have been turned on by the "language" in the book (which includes the illustrations). They are active rather than passive and their enthusiasm is contagious. Reading Judith Viorst's *Alexander and the Terrible, Horrible, No Good, Very Bad Day* silently is not nearly as engaging as listening to a teacher read it to a group of youngsters who are discovering the magic of language and comparing Alexander's day to theirs.

Prediction

Learners who have a difficult time with written language may not realize that as readers, part of their responsibility is to draw on their own experience in making sense out of what they are reading. Prediction is an effective way to encourage students to activate their prior knowledge. Before reading Maurice Sendak's *Where the Wild Things Are*, for example, the teacher asks, "What do you think this story is about?" But the children don't respond. Perhaps they are thinking, "Just tell us—we don't want to think—that's too hard."

    Teacher: *(thinking aloud)* Hmmm . . . Well, the first thing I'll do is read the title of the book, "Where the Wild Things Are." . . . Well, who wants to guess now?
    Students: *(no response).*
    Teacher: *(thinking aloud)* Well, the title didn't give me enough information, so I think I'll look at the picture on the cover. I see some trees and a funny-looking animal. He has a head that looks sort of like a buffalo, paws like a bear, and a very big body. There's also a ship in the ocean . . . Who wants to be brave and take a guess?
    Johnny: I think it's about animals.
    Mary: Maybe it's about a buffalo.
    Sue: I went to a circus once.
    Teacher: Any more guesses?
    Children all at one time: The circus, the zoo, a boy lost in the jungle.
    Teacher: Those are good guesses. Let's read and find out.

Now students are primed to listen, and they have a more specific sense of what the book will be about.

Cueing Systems

Most students with mild to moderate disabilities are able to demonstrate functional oral language. They are able to use all the linguistic cueing systems (pragmatic, semantic, syntactic, and phonic) with some degree of proficiency. Of course, children with severe language impairments need more time and more intense language demonstrations. Most of these learners understand how language works. What they need is help in understanding how reading and writing work through appropriate demonstrations of the interaction of the cueing systems in written language. When the teacher skims the text with her finger, for example, she is demonstrating that print and writing proceed from left to right and from top to bottom. As she points to each word, she is also demonstrating graphophonic relationships. To demonstrate how to use contextual clues to decode unknown words, she skips an "unknown" word. In Brenda Parkes's (1986) Big Book, *Who's in the Shed?*, for example, the teacher reads:

> "Let me have a peep,"
> baaed the big white sheep.
> "Let me have a peep."
> So the sheep had a peep
> through a hole in the shed.
> What did she see?

When the teacher reads the next verse, she demonstrates how to figure out an unknown word.

> "My turn now,"
> "m-m-m" . . .

The teacher stammers to indicate that she doesn't know the word "mooed." She thinks aloud, "Hmm, I don't know this word. I'll read on to see if I can figure out what word beginning with the letter *m* makes sense here.

> . . . the sleek brown cow.
> "My turn now."

Thinking aloud, the teacher says, "I'll go back and reread that sentence."

> "My turn now,"
> . . . the sleek brown cow.

The teacher thinks aloud, "What does a cow do that starts with *m*? . . . mmm, mah, moo. Oh, a cow moos." And she continues reading:

> "My turn now,"
> Moos the sleek brown cow
> "My turn now."
> So the cow had a peep through a hole in the shed.
> What did she see?

When the teacher and the students have read this story several times, the teacher might decide to conduct a quick mini-lesson:

I noticed some quotation marks before and after some of the words in the story. For example, there are quotation marks in the sentence "'Let me have a peep,' baaed the big white sheep." The quotation marks alert us that the words inside are what the sheep said. Can you find other examples in which quotation marks are used? I also noticed another mark that looks something like a backward *s*. Who can find one? It is called question mark. When you see a question mark, the author is telling you that a question is being asked.

Through this demonstration, students could see how written language works and how writers use punctuation to signal meaning. Within the context of the story, context clues and quotation and question marks become meaningful.

Demonstrations are illustrations of the problem-solving processes of readers and writers as they interact with written language. Meaningful demonstrations occur naturally in reading a text aloud. Students hear how good reading should sound, and if the teacher thinks aloud as well, they can eavesdrop on her thinking processes.

EXPECTATIONS

Frank Smith (1985) has observed that young learners actually think that they can learn anything—until someone or something convinces them otherwise. When students come to school, for example, they believe they will learn to read. But when their learning needs and the teacher's instruction are mismatched, they may not progress at the expected rate. Perhaps they are called "learning disabled," "reading delayed," "reading disabled," "mentally handicapped," or "dyslexic." Despite their hard work, repeated failure coupled with these negative labels send a strong message that they are not good readers or good students and are unlikely to succeed. They may get to the point where they actually expect to fail because it has always been that way. Teachers encourage them and urge them on ("Oh, just try a little harder . . . I know you can do it . . . you really are smart") but students with a history of failure believe that those are empty words. Who can blame them for thinking, "I've tried hard in the past and I still failed, so why try hard now? It's a lot easier to fail without trying than to fail after doing a lot of hard work."

A literacy program designed for students who have experienced few successes must accomplish two purposes: to prevent negative attributions from occurring, and shift any that have occurred in a more positive direction.

Statements that reflect negative attributions:

"I don't read/write well."
"I don't read/write well enough."
"I can't spell."
"I'm a slow reader/writer."
"You know I can't read/write that."
"Read/write it for me."

Children who make such statements do so because they have received these messages from their teachers or parents. To promote positive attributions and diminish negative messages, consider the following:

1. *Minimize the amount of correcting you do while a child is reading or writing.* Wait until the child has finished and then go back and talk about miscues, but not before highlighting what the child did correctly.

2. *Don't dwell on a child's "reading level."* (Reading level is an inaccurate comparison of the child to a sample group; see Chapter 7).

3. *Mix students with varying reading abilities.* Children quickly figure out that they are in the low reading group.

4. *Discuss a child's literacy abilities in terms of what the child is doing well, emerging skills, and goals.* Avoid a "can't do" perspective. Let students know that you will support their efforts. For example, one resource teacher commented to a fifth-grade student, "You made a terrific attempt in reading the information about rain forests. I noticed that when you had trouble recognizing the word 'environment' you skipped it and went on and then later you were able to figure it out. That was great! That's what good readers do. You're becoming a good reader."

The whole language philosophy expects students to learn, including those who have not learned in the past. Because of that expectation, we should make an effort to "catch them learning." If we provide the appropriate conditions, we must trust that they will learn.

RESPONSE

Brian Cambourne (1988) characterizes a whole language response to a learner's literacy development as *acceptance, celebration, evaluation,* and *demonstration.* To respond appropriately, the teacher makes decisions about the learner's development and progress based on several criteria. First, if a learner's literacy attempt is a true representation of what the learner can do, the teacher accepts it. If the attempt shows progress, she accepts it *and* celebrates it. What if there has only been an inkling of progress (skills are emerging), must she wait to celebrate until everything is just right? If a child shows progress, I think some celebration is always in order. Any step forward is reason for celebration. Since teachers who work with special learners have been trained to watch students' development and record it, they should not find it too difficult to decide how much celebration is warranted—and how much demonstration may still be needed.

Learners in special classes may show a little progress in their literacy attempts but still have many problems. A teacher must then be both supportive and constructive, focusing on what the learner is trying to read or communicate, not on "rightness" or "wrongness." This is the time to individualize demonstrations to fit the learner's needs.

Here is an example of how one teacher tried to make her individualized responses both supportive and constructive. Her intermediate resource class began to do research about reptiles after completing a unit on dinosaurs. They were in the process of writing about their research topics. After reading Susan's paragraph about lizards, her teacher said, "Your paragraph about lizards is a good first draft—you have included some very interesting facts. Now you need to put them together in a good paragraph form. All the sentences in one paragraph should be related. Let's work together to decide if all of your sentences meet this criteria." The teacher recognized that Susan was performing well and congratulated her. Then the teacher raised the expectation but gave Susan specific suggestions for meeting it.

The teacher also read Gary's paragraph about snakes. She complimented him on three sentences that were very good. Then she pointed out that two sentences were not complete and challenged him to find them and correct them. In this situation, the teacher recognized that Gary understood the concept of complete sentences and just needed a little nudge.

In another instance, this same teacher noticed that Brian was not writing much because he had difficulty spelling. She suggested, "For now, spell the words you don't know the way they sound or just put the beginning letter. We'll worry about the correct spelling later." The teacher recognized that Brian wasn't getting much accomplished and offered a temporary solution to ease his frustration and help him get some work done.

Charles (identified as mildly retarded with an IQ of 65) was placed in a fifth-grade classroom. The students were gathering in literature circles and were to choose from a selection of five books. Because all of them were too difficult for Charles to read independently, the special education teacher individualized his reading assignment for him, but without totally pulling him from the group. First, she pulled together the five students who were reading the same book. As a group they discussed the title and what they thought the book would be about. They also discussed chapter titles and what each chapter might be about. The teacher made sure Charles was included in the discussion. When the members of the group decided they wanted to read silently, the special education teacher and Charles went into the hall to discuss how he would like to read—silently or with her. Charles decided he would like the teacher to read aloud to him while he listened. For homework, he asked if his mother could read aloud to him and selected a book he could read independently to take home. The teachers and the students in that fifth-grade classroom sent several messages to Charles: you are a reader; you are part of the group; we respect you as an individual.

IN CLOSING

Making the classroom environment more learner-centered requires some adjustments in the teacher's behavior. The teacher becomes a facilitator and a supporter rather than a giver of information. The teacher thinks about how to immerse the students in written language through meaningful language activities. She provides appropriate demonstrations within the context of these language activities. She expects her students to learn, and she responds in a manner that clearly sends a message: "You are an active learner; you know a great deal; I will support your learning."

One Classroom Community

Students come to Pam Evans's resource room for anywhere from thirty minutes to three hours a day. Their ages range from six years to twelve years old, but somehow, in spite of the complexities of scheduling and their varied learning disabilities, she not only supports their academic growth but also structures the environment so that they learn to take responsibility for their own learning, to cooperate with others, to solve problems, and to respect each other.

As the children enter the classroom, the first thing they do is check the message board.

Things to Do:

1. Journal
2. Shared reading/writing
3. Work on play—"The Greatest Flying Machine"
4. Check bean plants—Record observations

Spelling:

Kim—Choose 3 words
John—Choose 5 words
Kris—Choose 4–6 words
Matt—Choose 5 words
Lew—Choose 5 words

Centers:

Books/Tapes
Reading by yourself or with buddy
Writing
Math Shelf
Jitters—Spelling game

Find a crazy poem and copy it for hallway display
Interview our guest

Today is December 2
Georges Seurat, a famous artist, was born in 1859. Question of the day:
    What is pointillism?

The children choose their work assignment and Pam talks with them about the day's events and the various items on the message board.

During one visit I learned about their "Work in Progress." Several pieces of chart paper filled with writing were hanging on the wall. This was a rough draft of a group story they were writing, "The Greatest Flying Machine." They had roughed out a story and their goal was to transform it into a play. They had already decided on the specific characters, the scenery, and the props. On this day they decided to have a group conference about how they would make their props. First, they discussed the flying machine:

John: I have an old bicycle we can use.
Jacob: I have a big wheel.
John: My mother might not let me use it.
Pam: Should we make the flying machine out of cardboard?
Jacob: Yeah, I have some I can bring.
Patrick: What about dust? What will we use for dust?

Dust became a major topic of conversation and suggestions flew:
baby powder
carpet sprinkle
crumbled up leaves
chalk dust
(No, some people are allergic to those things.)
confetti
paper punch holes
(That will make a big mess.)
(I can bring a dust buster.)

After a lengthy discussion of the pros and cons of these ideas, Pam asked, "How will we choose parts?" Kim quickly and matter-of-factly stated, "We will put all the parts and responsibilities in a hat and each person will draw." Pam replied, "That sounds fair. What do the rest of you think?" Everyone agreed.

Later, I discovered that performing plays was not new to these children. They often act out favorite books. In fact, they had made scenery from cardboard boxes and used it over and over. I'm not exactly sure when or how it was decided, but I was invited to be part of the audience for a dramatization of *Just This Once* by Joy Cowley (1993). I observed a great deal of problem solving during the preparations. Pam didn't overtly intrude on their planning, but she did act as a facilitator by asking questions such as, "How should the chairs be arranged for the audience?" Quickly the class members rearranged furniture so everyone in the audience would have a good view. Kim emerged as the director. She took responsibility for placing scenery and explaining to the actors that a narrator would read the parts between the actors' lines.

Each person retrieved appropriate "costumes" from the costume box and necessary props from the prop box. Dad wore a sweater vest, Mom wore beads, the daughter wore a blouse with a bow and carried a suitcase, and the hippo crouched behind a cardboard cutout. It was interesting to note that the players were oblivious to gender. John, for example, played the part of the daughter. The remaining students sat in the audience and responded appropriately. A second production was quickly assembled to give everyone a chance to participate.

During the day I watched as the process of play production moved through various stages. What I observed was much more than kids having fun "play acting." Pam had discovered that her students enjoyed creative dramatics, and she drew on this enthusiasm to encourage collaboration, cooperation, problem solving, and risk taking in a meaningful context. I also noticed that the children were very accepting of one another. They all seemed to share the underlying assumption that they would each participate in the manner of their choice. They disregarded "shortcomings," since quality of performance wasn't their main goal. Their major concern was the satisfaction of creating and participating. What I observed was a truly democratic classroom community.

Many strategies and activities complement a whole language philosophy, but mere engagement in such activities does not necessarily establish a learning environment that supports a whole language philosophy. The "heart and soul" of a learner-centered classroom is the creation of a democratic classroom community. James Beane and Michael Apple (1995) describe a democratic classroom as one in which children have a sense of shared purpose and work toward common goals through cooperation and collaboration. Teacher and students respond to each other's concerns, aspirations, and interests. However, it is not "engineered consent" to something the teacher has planned in advance. Students are encouraged to express their own ideas and opinions. Most important, diversity is viewed not as a problem but as a valuable resource.

A democratic classroom community includes three basic elements:

1. The *teacher,* who is key because he or she has settled on establishing a democratic classroom community as a philosophical choice. By virtue of this choice, the teacher

   - is a facilitator, not a control agent.
   - assumes responsibility for identifying students' learning strengths and emerging skills, as well as areas that need support.
   - provides appropriate learning experiences that engage students.

2. An *environment* that

   - nurtures learning in a social context through collaboration and cooperation.
   - encourages risk taking.
   - accommodates learning preferences through individual choice.
   - respects individual development.

3. *Learners,* who have learned or are in the process of learning

   - to respect one another's uniqueness, cultural background, physical attributes, and diverse abilities.
   - to be responsible for their own learning.
   - to work without fear of ridicule, rejection or failure.
   - to cooperate with others.

It is easy to observe these elements in Stephanie Jacob's classroom. At a certain time of day, children are scattered around the room in what appears to be a "nonlearning" time. At first glance, it seems unstructured and somewhat chaotic: two girls perch at a table conferring about a story they are writing; in a corner two boys read a book together, laughing and talking about the really good parts; another group is gathered at a reading chart (one student plays teacher by pointing to the words as the other students read along. Then another student takes over as teacher).

In reality, Stephanie's classroom community has a great deal of structure. While there may be freedom to collaborate, to move around, and to make choices, this "freedom" has parameters. They are defined by class rules, class goals, individual goals, and respect for individual rights. Stephanie works hard to orchestrate the classroom climate by helping each child have a sense of belonging; organizing a social context for learning; and encouraging the development of responsibility and independence.

BELONGING

Lisa, a special education teacher who attended a summer class I taught, invited me to visit her class—"Come anytime," she said. One October day, when I had finished visiting a student teacher, I happened to drive by Lisa's school. On the spur of the moment I decided to accept her invitation. I stopped by the office for directions to her resource room, but I didn't go in immediately. First I wanted to soak up everything that was posted on the wall outside: a large welcome sign and a picture of each student next to which was a collage that I assumed represented favorite foods, movie stars, sports heros, singers, and so on. As I entered the classroom I no longer felt that I was visiting a class; rather, I was entering a community that called itself "The Giants."

When I stepped inside, a young man noticed me. He quickly came up to me, introduced himself as Roy, and welcomed me to the class. Lisa then introduced me to everyone. She asked Roy if he would like to take me on a tour of the room. During the tour I noticed the name and picture of the student of the week displayed prominently on the front bulletin board and a rotating job chart: today, Roy was Lisa's helper. I also noticed a student straightening the books in the reading center. When I glanced at the job chart to see if I could discover who he might be, I didn't see that particular job listed. I asked him what his job was, and he explained that today he was in charge of taking the lunch count. When I complimented him for straightening the books, he just shrugged his shoulders, "We always keep our classroom neat."

Relationships

Denise, a teacher of students identified as behaviorally disordered, established a sense of belonging in her classroom by having her students list five to ten things about themselves they wanted to share with someone in the class. Next, with a partner, they read each other's lists and responded. For example, Joe, one of her high school students, wrote:

1. I am a very nice person.
2. I love motorcycles.
3. I am kind of funny.
4. I am trying to quit smoking.
5. I love comic books.
6. I like working with wood.

Joe and Sara then shared lists. The result was the following written conversation.

Sara: What things do you say that are funny?
Joe: I make impressions.
Sara: How old were you when you started smoking?
Joe: Ten.
Sara: Why did you start smoking in the first place?
Joe: Because I wanted to.
Sara: What do you do with wood?
Joe: I make soapbox cars and birdhouses and model planes.

This written conversation acted as an icebreaker between two students who did not know each other. Joe was able to communicate things about himself he wanted to share (personal attributes: *nice person, funny;* interests: *motorcycles, comic books, woodworking;* a goal: *quit smoking*), the kind of information students might not find out about each other during class activities. Now the relationship between Joe and Sara has grown from merely sharing a class to sharing a sense of themselves.

Appreciating and Accepting Diversity

Children in public schools are becoming more and more diverse. By the twenty-first century, half of the school-age children in the United States will be children of color. Learning about different cultures and different family configurations should be encouraged. Like literacy, an understanding and appreciation of human diversity must be developed, and here too, immersion, demonstration, and meaningful engagement serve as useful techniques. The classroom environment and daily learning activities can encompass all areas of diversity: ethnicity, race, social class, disability, gender, and so on. (Wortis and Hall 1990).

To immerse students in an awareness of diversity, display pictures and photographs of

- multicultural events
- children of many cultures
- women in nontraditional roles
- active older people
- people working in different occupations
- people from diverse cultures wearing contemporary dress
- people of many nationalities and cultures engaged in family activities

To provide demonstrations and experiences of different cultures, explore

- art and music
- cooking

- creative dramatics
- "dressing up" in work clothes of all kinds in preschool and kindergarten
- studying various modes of shelter, such as tents, hogans, pueblos, pagodas

Teachers and children can also take advantage of the wealth of multicultural picture books, folktale collections, and novels that portray and validate minority and ethnic cultures (for a review of multicultural literature, see Cox and Galda 1990).

Although students spend a great deal of time in the classroom, they may not feel a genuine sense of belonging in what is, in fact, a "contrived" community. The teacher can enhance each student's sense of belonging by deliberately creating an environment in which every child has ownership and participates as a viable member. Class members can share each other's interests and cultural backgrounds through class projects, which can also encourage group cohesiveness.

A SOCIAL CONTEXT FOR LEARNING

Because a whole language philosophy integrates aspects of holistic, psychological, and social research, a major tenet of this philosophy is that learning should occur through collaboration and cooperation. As Halliday (1978) and others have pointed out, humans are by nature social: they want to share experiences and insights through language. Research shows that social interaction and cooperative learning experiences increase both individual cognitive development and individual emotional development (Doise and Mugny 1984; Johnson et al. 1981). The positive results of social learning experiences are many:

- deeper understanding of topics of study
- different points of view
- new knowledge
- opportunities for learners to develop leadership roles
- more positive attitudes toward school
- positive peer relationships
- acceptance of disabilities and diversity

I first introduced Margaret Glass in Chapter 3, where I described her classroom as well as her feelings and thoughts about whole language. Several years have passed since she began exploring whole language as a foundation for her curriculum. I still visit her classroom several times a year, and each year I observe her growth. She reinforces my observations in her own accounts of the changes she has made. She says she is more structured now, but "that's good." My own perception is that she is simply more self-confident about arranging the classroom learning environment to support potential growth. The "structure" comes from knowing what she wants to happen and how to make it happen. Carefully observing her students' development over the past few years has given her the confidence to trust her students and to allow natural collaborative situations.

When Margaret showed me her students' writing accomplishments in their journals, what I heard was not just an account of their drawings, scribbles, and stories but her confident expectations of what was to come.

We've been in school about two months. At the beginning of the year this child didn't want to scribble; he didn't want to draw. Within days he began both scribbling and drawing. Then he began making a few letters. He's starting to copy words from books. Soon, he will be writing words on his own and sentences. He's going to just take off!

The children write in their journals the first thing in the morning, as soon as they come into the classroom. Before long they are all writing. As I moved among the students, I observed two boys with their heads together, talking quietly. Margaret explained how this alliance had occurred. Six-year-old Chris knew that eight-year-old Michael could spell words and often asked for Michael's assistance, which Michael willingly gave. Over time, they became collaborators. They share their writing with each other and exchange ideas.

Collaboration occurs naturally throughout the day because of the way Margaret structures learning activities. She often draws on seasonal events for literacy experiences. She reads aloud a variety of genres, from storybooks and poetry to nonfiction. The children then pool their knowledge to create informational charts. As they verbalize their ideas, Margaret acts as secretary and records their words on chart paper. These charts are visited daily and new information is added. Here is a sample:

Thanksgiving is in November. It is on the fourth Thursday. The Native Americans and the Pilgrims celebrated Thanksgiving together. We eat turkey at Thanksgiving.

Margaret also attends to students' interests in setting up theme studies. During the Halloween theme study, for example, the students became intrigued with the moon. To help satisfy their curiosity, Margaret brought books about the moon from the library. Eventually, the class carried out an in-depth study of space.

The children in Margaret's class feel a sense of security. The days have a predictable format: journal writing and individual reading, free choice, calendar time, read aloud, shared reading, writing workshop, math, and theme study. At the same time, Margaret has designed these daily events so that she and the children can write and talk about their experiences and insights in a respectful, accepting environment.

Cooperative Learning

If collaboration is a less formalized means of social learning, cooperative learning is usually distinguished by a common effort toward a group goal that requires individual accountability, collaboration, and group processing skills (Kagan 1985; Slavin 1983). Cooperative learning has proven to be an effective technique not only in boosting academic achievement but also in increasing self-esteem and encouraging positive attitudes toward others, including individuals with disabilities (Sharan 1980; Johnson and Johnson 1989; Slavin 1990). A growing body of research indicates that cooperative learning can be effective in heterogeneous classes as an alternative to ability grouping, remedial pullouts, and separate special education classes (Stevens and Slavin 1992).

In reviewing the effects of cooperative learning, Robert Slavin (1990) concluded that two conditions were especially important for increased achievement: first, some type of group goal or reward, such as a certificate or some other type of recognition; and second, individual contributions to group success. The group, in other words, must be a community of learners who see it as their role to help their groupmates learn. This kind of group support has the potential to help individuals achieve beyond their actual ability level through guidance and collaboration (L. S. Vygotsky's [1978] "zone of proximal development").

Group Skills

Working cooperatively in groups allows children to learn about gender, other cultures, and diverse abilities. It is vitally important that learners with disabilities who will be included in general education classes know how to work in group situations. Group work will not be successful unless all students have basic group skills:

- making space for everyone
- staying with the group
- using quiet voices
- calling each other by name
- making eye contact
- taking turns
- listening well
- avoiding "put downs"
- negotiating conflict
- reaching consensus

As a K–5 resource teacher, Pam Evans began collaborating with a fourth-grade general education teacher to mainstream five resource students into the "regular" social studies class. The two teachers decided to try cooperative learning, but before long, they discovered that *all* the children needed to learn how to work cooperatively. They decided to begin with mini-lessons on topics such as what cooperation is, how to make room, how to listen during conversation, and how to use "buildups" rather than "put-downs." In one lesson, the teachers demonstrated good and poor listening behaviors and asked students to identify the good behaviors. In another, the children made a comparison chart of "buildups" and "put-downs."

Buildups	*Put-downs*
You're a nice person.	That's a stupid question.
I'm glad you're here.	You talk funny.
You're good at riding a bike.	Ha-ha, you can't ride a bike.
You're my friend.	You're not my friend anymore.
You're super.	You eat grass.

According to Pam, the one-hour coteaching experience with the social studies class has made a world of difference in how the class perceives her and her resource students. Because she takes equal responsibility in teaching, students see her as a "real" teacher.

Susan Hill and Timothy Hill (1990) suggest that after the students have worked in groups for a while, teachers should look at what is working and what is not. For example, if a group is having difficulty taking turns, the teacher might sit with two competent turn takers and discuss a topic—what they did over the weekend, for example. The role players sit in the center while the rest of the class sits in a circle or semi-circle watching.

Another effective demonstration of appropriate skills is the problem-solving exercise I call "Take two." The teacher prepares a script depicting inappropriate group behavior that results in a breakdown of group performance (an argument, someone leaving the group, and so on). At some point near the end of the "drama," the teacher calls out, "Stop the camera!" and the actors stop. Next the class discusses why the breakdown occurred. The teacher asks those in the audience to brainstorm ways the breakdown might have been avoided. When they have reached a consensus about appropriate behavior, the teacher says, "Take two," and the actors replay the scene according to audience suggestions.

These types of activities are good demonstrations of how groups should work. The more demonstrations children see and the more opportunities they have to practice group skills, the better they will get. Learners shouldn't miss out on group work just because they don't perform well in the beginning. They need to practice it, like any other skill, in a meaningful context. Likewise, if students are expected to perform a specific job in a group, they must understand how to do the job. Here, again, role playing can help students understand what the expectations are.

Whole language classrooms promote learning through social interaction. Collaboration and cooperative learning encourage positive academic results as well as positive peer relationships, including an acceptance of diversity. These approaches may not be successful, however, if the teacher does not provide an appropriate environment, how-to demonstrations, and ample opportunities to collaborate and cooperate in contexts relevant to learners' needs.

IN CLOSING

In a democratic learning community members consider and treat each other as equals. Because members have a vested interest in their own personal learning and in the learning of their fellow classmates, they experience what it is like to be responsible and contributing community participants. When students have choices, and shared goals as well as their own independent goals, when collaboration and cooperation are demonstrated and encouraged, a learning environment and a community of learners can evolve.

While a "democratic classroom" might seem to be an oxymoron (Beane and Apple 1995), it shouldn't be. As Deborah Meir and Paul Schwarz (1995) point out, if a primary goal of public schools is to educate productive citizens, they should be places where children can experience democracy. After all, one doesn't learn to play a game if one has never seen it.

Evaluation from a Whole Language Perspective

P.L. 94-142 requires special education teachers to document achievement beyond traditional grading and standardized achievement tests. Processing a student through special education services involves appropriate assessment procedures. First, an intensive evaluation determines whether a student meets eligibility requirements. If a child is eligible, results from assessment procedures are used by a multidisciplinary team to develop an Individual Education Program (IEP) and to monitor the student's progress annually as long as the student receives special services. This chapter discusses assessment procedures that are compatible with a whole language philosophy. (Chapter 8 looks in more detail at how assessment data can be used to respond to individual needs through portfolios and IEPs.)

TRADITIONAL ASSESSMENT

The classroom is a small community within the larger communities of the school district, the civic community, the state, and the nation as a whole. This means there are a number of people besides educators and parents who have a stake in the education of children and youth. The primary stakeholders are the learners, parents, and teachers, and they want information relevant to the learner's progress and instruction in the cognitive, affective, and social domains. The secondary stakeholders may include school administrators, state and federal agencies, and politicians, all of whom seek comparative data: How well are the students in my school achieving compared to those in other schools in the district? How well are the students in my state achieving compared to those in other states? How well are the children and youth of our country achieving compared to those in other industrial nations?

For the most part, educational assessment responds to the needs of secondary stakeholders rather than those of primary stakeholders. The types of assessment that carry the most weight with secondary stakeholders are some sort of "formal" achievement assessment, such as standardized tests, or, to a lesser degree, textbook mastery tests, curriculum-based assessment, or published criterion-referenced tests. These procedures do indeed produce comparative data, but they are of limited value in making instructional decisions and do not respond adequately to the needs of primary stakeholders.

"Formal" assessment techniques such as standardized tests and scales have limited instructional value because they have been prepared in advance and reflect the values and biases of those who developed them (Poplin 1984). Test items may not reflect the actual classroom curriculum. In addition, only certain answers are considered correct, and little leeway is given to the judgment of the examiner. An example: Ben, a student receiving services in a resource room, was being evaluated in an annual review of his progress. He was given a test, one item of which asked the meaning of the word "strapped," as in the sentence, "John is strapped." The "correct" answer according to the test is that "John doesn't have any money." Ben, however, defined "strapped" as "wearing a gun," which is correct according to current slang. The examiner understands that it is a plausible interpretation given the limited context, but according to the scoring procedures, the examiner cannot give Ben credit for this answer.

Often the standardized tests used to judge progress may be poor reflections of the student's actual progress. Michael's score on a standardized spelling test indicated that he had not made any progress, yet when the teacher compared his previous test protocol with his current test protocol, she was able to point out a great amount of progress: He had spelled almost correctly words he did not even attempt the previous year. She was very proud of his "invented" spelling because he was taking risks, and it was evident what words he was attempting to spell. Of course he did not receive credit for any of the almost correctly spelled words; in fact, his raw score was only two points higher than the previous year. This is a classic example of how little a score reveals about the learning that has taken place.

Finally, tests may not assess skills in a valid manner. For efficiency, tests often rely on multiple-choice items. But this format may not be an appropriate procedure for measuring certain skills. For instance, *The Peabody Individual Achievement Test-Revised* (Markwardt 1989) requires the examinee to choose the correct spelling of a word from a list. This, of course, does not represent the authentic application of spelling skills in real life. The test also asks the examinee to read aloud single words in isolation. But this procedure robs the examinee of linguistic cues (syntax, semantics, pragmatics), which learners routinely use to make meaning while reading.

Achievement tests have been elevated to a pedestal because they are assumed to be objective and accurate. Consumers, however, should be aware they they may be neither.

What Scores Tell Us

Standardized tests produce many scores: grade and age equivalent scores, standard scores, percentile rank, and stanines, all of which are intended to tell us how an individual student compares to the normed sample of the test.

Grade and age equivalent scores are commonly used—and often misused. An age equivalent score means that an individual's raw score is the average (mean or median) raw score for the normed age group. Similarly, a grade equivalent score means that a raw score is the average (mean or median) performance for that grade. Perhaps the average score for the normed group for eight-year-olds is 30. According to these data, any individual who takes the test and receives a raw score of 30 will receive the age equivalent score of eight years. (We should remember that in order to get a mean or a median score, many will be above or below the average.) Age and grade equivalent scores are appealing because the concept is concrete and appears to be easy to undersand (Venn 1994). Yet Salvia and Ysseldyke (1981) point out four problems with equivalent scores:

1. A student who earns an age equivalent of 8.0 years has correctly answered the same number of questions as the average of all eight-year-olds in the normed population of the test. This does not mean that the student performed exactly like an eight-year-old. Perhaps a younger child who scored the same as the average eight-year-old has performed lower-level work with greater accuracy, while an older child who received this score attempted more problems (the younger may have correctly answered 40 out of 48 attempted, and the older child correctly answered 40 out of 70 attempted).

2. Incremental age and grade scores (for example, 8 years, 6 months; 4.5 grade level) are estimated for groups of children who are never tested: the average score of each age group and grade-placement group is plotted on a graph; the lines on the graph are extended (extrapolated) at both extremes to account for the scores below and above the averages found. In addition, grade placements are stated in tenths of a school year. The grade equivalent score of 7.2 means the second year of the seventh grade. Age equivalents are stated in years and months. If a raw score falls beween the averages of the age or grade (for example between 6 years and 7 years) the raw score would be estmated as 6 years 6 months even though no children 6 years 6 months were tested.

3. The use of these types of scores reinforces typological thinking. For example, the average 8.0-year-old does not really exist; the average of 8.0 represents a range. In addition, if we think of average performance as the mean or median score, we are saying that about 50 percent of the population perform below average.

4. Age and grade equivalent scores are ordinal data, which rank scores as having a higher or a lower value. Intervals between adjacent scores are not equal. This means that the difference between the highest score and the next highest is not the same as the difference between the second highest score and the third highest (100, 98, 94, 90, 82): the scores are not at equal intervals.

These problems are inherent in any type of assessment that gives age or grade equivalencies. Some test developers and publishers realize the inherent problems of age and grade equivalency scores and do not provide such scores. But many publishers continue to provide them because consumers want them. Caution must also be used with criterion-referenced, mastery tests and curriculum-based assessments, because mastery levels may be arbitrarily set (Johnston 1992; Valencia and Pearson 1988).

"Formal" assessment procedures are not perfect and may in fact present distorted information about actual student achievement. This type of assessment should be put into perspective and not given undo weight. When too much emphasis is put on the results of such tests, the curriculum is at risk for being assessment driven rather than learner driven.

Special Education Assessment

When discussing assessment procedures with veteran special education teachers I hear the same comments over and over:

> I give the "X" test and write the results down because I have to. When I confer with parents I don't discuss the test results because I don't think they are valid.

> Sometimes the test scores are lower than last year's! I know my students learned something.

> We use this test because the school district spent a lot of money on the computerized version.

> My students' spelling has really improved. Last year Billy had no idea of sound-symbol relationship; now he is spelling words as they sound, and I can read his work.

> The problem is that the test we use to document progress doesn't consider inventive spelling. It just simply doesn't show the real progress my students have made.

What I hear in these comments is frustration, not that evaluation is meaningless but that the method teachers are using is neither useful nor positive. The reason for this frustration, I suggest, is that the theory base of the assessment instruments does not match the teachers' theory of learning.

The IEP, mandated for students in special education by P. L. 94-142, has created some assessment misconceptions. The IEP was designed with good intentions, like an educational insurance policy, to broadly define annual goals and specific short-term objectives for the student and describe how progress toward these goals and objectives will be evaluated. This is all well and good, but it makes several assumptions when applied in the traditional manner. First, it assumes that we can and should state in advance what students should learn, how well they will learn it, and approximately when they should learn it. As a result, short-term goals and methods of evaluation may look like the following:

> Student will demonstrate adding numbers involving two renamings by computing 20 addition problems requiring two renamings with 80 percent accuracy.

If the student has accomplished the objective as stated, according to this method the student has made progress. If not, reteaching and/or practice will occur until the student achieves the criterion. This process is known as *diagnostic-prescriptive* or *clinical teaching*. An implied assumption is that if anything not stated as an objective on the IEP is learned, it is not significant.

Second, it is assumed that the stated objectives are appropriate. In many instances IEP objectives come from standardized tests, criterion-referenced tests, curriculum-based assessment, and textbook mastery tests. These assessment methods are assumed to be objective and accurate measures of knowledge and achievement. In addition, these assessments are typically divided into subtests, such as mathematics calculation, mathematics reasoning, reading recognition, and reading comprehension. This method of organization simplifies the process of discerning so-called strengths and weaknesses. The areas in which a student performs below average are considered weaknesses from which objectives can then be written; instruction is based on meeting these objectives. Such myopic assessment of achievement results in a deficit model of instruction. It underestimates strengths and ignores or discounts learning that occurs in other areas.

HOLISTIC EVALUATION

Holistic evaluation attempts to view the learner and learning as a whole (Keefe 1993). From this perspective evaluation becomes a matter of systematically putting together information that has been gathered from multiple sources—observation of students in authentic learning situations, work samples, interviews and conferences with students. The key element is the willingness to see and hear the unexpected and listen to one's intuition. Robert Stake (1975) describes it as "responsive" evaluation. It is an attempt to gather information from a variety of sources and contexts in order to respond to the concerns of primary as well as secondary stakeholders.

Observation

Although teachers observe their students all the time, they may not take time to record pertinent information. This kind of record-keeping, however, is crucial, because it is easy to forget how a child was performing and behaving three months ago. The trick is to develop a systematic method for keeping track of observations. It should be efficient and not too complicated.

Some teachers like to keep an observation notebook, divided so that there are three to five blank pages for each child; others prefer to jot quick notes with dates. Some teachers categorize their notes according to content areas, skill areas, strategies, and perhaps IEP goals.

Observation of students in the learning environment should be ongoing. I suggest that teachers make two lists to reflect two kinds of observation: "Things I Know I Want to Know" and "Aha" (things I didn't know I wanted to know—the unexpected). First, take some time to think about some questions you would like to answer:

- What kind of language control does the student have? (e.g., able to listen attentively, make requests, retell an event, ask questions for clarification, etc.)
- What is the student's attitude toward reading? (e.g., engages in reading

voluntarily, reads for a variety of purposes, talks about what he/she has read)
- What does the student choose to read? (fiction, nonfiction, magazines)
- What kind of reading strategies does the student use? (activates schema, picture clues, context clues)
- What does the student demonstrate about writing? (e.g., knows the purpose of writing, writes about a variety of topics, stays on topic, uses mechanical conventions)
- What kind of learning strategies does the student use? (organization, time management, sources for help)

These questions are obviously just suggestions to get teachers thinking about the different things that can be observed in a variety of contexts. It is impossible to observe all children in every situation; a teacher should concentrate on one or two students at a time, developing a schedule that allows for a focused observation for each student during one month or an entire grading period.

Observing Learners in a Large Group

When observing learners during whole or large group instruction, notice whether or not they attend to the group activity. Does the learner engage in group discussion or volunteer to answer questions? Or does the learner rely on peer support for learning? (Diane, for example, does not participate in the group discussion, but she does listen to what others say.)

Observing Learners in a Small Group

A small group setting allows more specific questions: Does the learner emerge as a group leader? Does the learner cooperate with peers? Does the learner take more risks in a small group than in a large group? Does the learner ask for assistance or take the role of teacher?

Observing Learners as They Work Independently

A good time to observe how learners apply learning strategies is while they work on their own. One teacher overheard a student saying, "Kitchen begins with a *k*—oh yeah, like in K-Mart." The student was using a familiar logo to trigger his memory.

"Aha" Observations

"Aha" observations are concurrent with "I Want to Know" observations and reflect skills and insights that were not part of the focused observation. This list acknowledges the unanticipated learning taking place.

Both types of observation generate what I call a "Can Do" list, a record of the skills, strategies, and knowledge the learner has demonstrated. It should also reflect emerging skills. Sharing the "Can Do" list with learners and their parents establishes a positive, supportive tone and provides assurance that learning is indeed taking place (see Figure 7.1).

Sometimes it may prove necessary to interview students in order to clarify

---

THINGS I WANT TO KNOW

2/13
Answered many questions during science class. Stayed on topic. Becoming more independent. I don't hear "I don't know how" as much anymore.

2/14
Made a semantic map to study for history test. Handwriting and spelling skills are improving. Realized "mabe" was misspelled.

2/15
During SSR read and article from *Glamour* magazine. At the beginning of the year she only glanced through magazines.

"AHA"

2/13
Desk is always neat and organized. I heard her refuse to let a friend copy from her homework.

2/14
She enjoys drawing pictures of animals.

2/15
Very cooperative. She changed center activity to accommodate a new student.

CAN DO

Answer questions
Stay on topic
Make semantic map as study aid
Recognize misspelled words
Read independently
Be neat and organized
Resist peer pressure
Draw
Be cooperative

EMERGING

Independence
Handwriting
Spelling

FIGURE 7.1 "Can Do" list records strategies, demonstrated knowledge, and emerging skills

an observation. An unstructured interview, which may be conducted anywhere and without a specific outcome in mind, is one way to do this. Questions such as, "Tell me about ———," "What do you like best about ———," or "How would you like to change ———?" (Searfoss 1994).

Conferences

Conferences are an invaluable method of taking the pulse of an entire classroom as well as of individual students. Lynn Rhodes and Curtis Dudley-Marling (1988) describe several kinds:

Roving

The teacher moves quickly around the room from individuals to groups asking how things are going and if anyone has questions. The teacher does not stop for in-depth discussion but tries to get an overall perspective of how students are doing and who might need more attention (Turnbill 1983).

Group

The teacher works with several students at a time, an effective method when several students are reading the same text or experiencing similar difficulties.

Whole Class

This conference takes the form of a five- to ten-minute mini-lesson if the teacher discovers that a majority of the students seem to be having similar problems or are asking similar questions. Students who are not having difficulty may provide assistance.

Peer

Consultation and collaboration among peers is an efficient and effective instructional strategy; however, it does not produce much assessment information for the teacher.

Sometimes teachers feel overwhelmed trying to address the needs of students during individual conferences. Deanna Wade, a teacher of primary behavioral disordered students, makes these conferences more manageable by setting up a schedule. She blocks out part of a specific day in five-, ten-, or fifteen-minute intervals (depending on the amount of time available). If students want to confer, they sign up for one of the available time periods. This method is effective because students know they have only a certain amount of time they can conference with their teacher. When their time is up, they relinquish their conference seat to the next child on the list. Students know that they will each get a turn, and Deanna can more easily remember which children have had an individual conference with her.

Conference Questions

Obviously, managing conference time is important, but getting specific information from a conference can also be a challenge. To elicit information from the students the teacher needs to ask both general and specific questions. Here are some examples:

Reading Conferences

- I see you've just started a new book. What do you think it is about?
- How's your reading going? Is this book (story) hard or easy for you?
- Tell me about one of the characters in the story.
- What's your favorite part of the story so far?
- Who is your favorite character?
- What would you do if (an event in the story) happened to you?
- What do you think (character in the story) could have done differently?
- Did you like the way the story ended? Would you end it differently?

Writing Conferences

- Who will read this story?
- What do you know a lot about?
- Do you know someone like the character in your story?
- This part sounds interesting—can you tell me more about it?

- Pretend I know nothing about this topic. What would you need to tell me about it?
- Which part are you having trouble with? How can I help?
- What questions would you like to ask me?
- What do you want your reader to know? feel?

Reading Evaluations

Interest Inventories

An interest inventory can provide a wealth of information about the learners in your classroom. This information is a good guide to use in selecting books, magazines, and other reading material for the reading center (see Figure 7.2).

Book lists

Invite students to keep an ongoing list of the books they read. This list can document quantity and indicate a reluctant reader's change in attitude toward reading.

Running Record of Reading Growth

A "running record" (Clay 1985) is a graphic record of oral reading that allows the teacher to compare a child's earlier and later reading performance. As the student reads aloud (or later, from a tape recording), the teacher records oral reading behaviors on a blank sheet of paper. The teacher does not need a copy of the text to write on, which makes this system flexible and downplays the sense of a "testing" situation (Johnston 1992).

A running record supplies both quantitative and qualitative data. Quantitative data includes error rate, accuracy rate, and a self-correction ratio. These data are useful if IEPs require numerical measures. Analyze errors to determine how the reader is using three linguistic cueing systems: semantics, syntax, and graphophonics. Such analysis can reveal whether the reader is using a balance of information from all three cueing systems or whether the reader is overusing or underusing certain cues.

Cloze Procedures

Cloze procedures are designed to evaluate a reader's ability to use prior knowledge and context clues to figure out unknown words. The reader completes a text that has a missing word or words. If the reader is able to fill in the blank with a word that makes sense, it is assumed that the reader is using prior knowledge and context clues.

The *Keefe Inventory of Silent Reading* (KISR; D. Keefe 1993) employs a cloze procedure to assess the reading strategies a child uses during silent reading. The instrument provides information similar to an oral reading inventory, but it has two advantages: it can be group administered and it reflects silent reading strategies. This inventory focuses on *forward referencing* (reading ahead of the deletion to obtain information) or *backward referencing* (reviewing what has

ABOUT ME

My name is _____ Date _____

THINGS I LIKE TO DO
1. On the weekends I like to _____
_____
2. After school I like to _____
_____
3. In the summer I like to _____
_____
4. My hobbies are _____

TV SHOWS AND MOVIES
5. Do you like to watch TV? _____
6. My favorite TV shows are _____
_____
7. Who is your favorite TV actor? _____
8. Do you like to watch movies? _____
9. What is your favorite movie or movies? _____
_____
10. Who is your favorite movie actor? _____

MUSIC
11. Do you like to listen to music? _____
12. Do you like to watch music videos? _____
13. What kind of music do you like? _____
14. What is your favorite song? _____
15. Who is your favorite singer? _____
16. What is your favorite music group? _____
17. What is your favorite musical instrument? _____

READING
18. Do you like to read for fun? _____
19. What is the title of a book you like? _____
20. Do you have a favorite author? _____
21. What kinds of things do you like to read?
    newspapers   magazines   comic books   books
22. What do you like to read about?
    animals   cars   sports   history
    famous people   romance   nature   make-believe
    science fiction other _____

SCHOOL
23. Do you like school? _____
24. What is your favorite subject? _____
25. What is your least favorite subject? _____

WHEN I GROW UP
26. I want to be a _____ when I grow up.
27. To do this I will need to learn _____

OTHER THINGS ABOUT ME
_____
_____
_____
_____
_____

FIGURE 7.2   An interest inventory contains a wealth of information about a student

been read). In addition it offers information about the reader's use of semantic, syntactic, and graphophonic cues.

The KISR (D. Keefe 1993) is designed to answer the following questions:

1. Does the reader use context cues by

    - backward referencing?
    - forward referencing?

2. Does the reader use semantic cues by paying attention to the meaning of the phrase, sentence, and/or the passage in which the blank appears?
3. Does the reader use syntactic cues by putting words that represent the same part of speech in the blanks provided?
4. Does the reader use graphophonic cues by paying attention to the initial letters in a word?
5. Does the reader activate schema (prior knowledge) when reading?
6. Does the reader take risks while reading and skip blanks when he or she is unable to fill them in without lengthy stopping and pondering?
7. Does the reader self-correct when he or she has filled in the blank with an inappropriate word?
8. Does the reader demonstrate persistence by continuing to try to fill blanks in even thought the task is becoming more difficult?
9. Does the reader read fluently, or does the reader's very slow reading rate prolong the task for an inordinate amount of time?

The teacher answers these questions by examining the inserted words or observing the amount of time the reader takes to complete the inventory.

This particular cloze procedure is unique in that it paraphrases the material from Mark Twain's *The Adventures of Tom Sawyer* at various levels of difficulty. The story opens at a beginning reading level and continues on through several levels of increasing difficulty. The student is instructed to fill in missing words: the words the reader provides do not have to be exact, but they should serve the same grammatical function as the intended words and be semantically acceptable. Replacement words that are not the same as the intended ones are called miscues and categorized according to the degree of grammatical and semantic acceptability (from minimal to very severe).

Sample passage:

> Aunt Polly was angry with Tom for telling her a lie. Tom had to lose his Saturday fun and stay home. He had to whitewash the fence in front of the———.

Although the intended word is *house,* the insertion of the word *yard* would be considered a minimal miscue because it is grammatically and semantically acceptable. However, nonsensical insertions such as "lepp" are not semantically, syntactically, or graphophonically acceptable. They indicate that the reader is not making sense of the passage.

Retelling

Learners' comprehension of written text is typically assessed by asking questions about the story they have read. This technique, however, does not elicit a sense of the learner's understanding of the text; it merely determines whether learners can answer the questions correctly. An alternative procedure is to ask learners to retell the story in their own words. Because predetermined comprehension questions may ask a reader to remember facts or incidents the reader didn't attend to, retelling is a more authentic method of finding out what the reader did comprehend. Retelling is especially effective for poor readers and for learners who have difficulty answering questions.

Before they read a passage, students should be told that they will be asked to retell it and what they should include in the retelling (major points, major characters, sequence of events, and so on). The following guidelines support a retelling (Morrow 1985):

Ask the child to retell the story by saying, "A little while ago you read the story [name of the story]. Would you tell the story as if you were telling it to a friend who has never heard it before?" If necessary, use a prompt such as "Once there was . . ." If the child stops before the end of the story, encourage her to continue by asking, "What comes next?" If the child seems to be having difficulty in continuing the story, use a prompt such as, "Did Jack run into trouble after he climbed the beanstalk?" For a learner experiencing a great deal of difficulty, it might be necessary to ask specific questions, such as, "Who is the story about?" "When did the story happen?" "Where did the story happen?" It is a good idea to record prompts for future reference. To analyze the retellings and collect data over time, a rating scale such as that in Figure 7.3 can be used.

Observing Silent Reading

While students are engaged in silent reading, observe whether a student displays the following *behaviors:*

- chooses books of a particular difficulty level
- shows a willingness to read
- stays on or off task
- scans book or reads book
- moves eyes
- maintains a level of concentration
- stays engaged for a length of time

Attitude Toward Reading

Similarly, assess a student's *attitude* about reading by observing certain behaviors:

- voluntarily reads during free time
- checks out books from the classroom or school library
- discusses reading with others
- participates in book clubs
- reads at home as reported by parents
- reads independently
- is willing to read aloud
- enjoys being read to
- consults other sources to get information about reading topic
- selects books because of theme, author, or recommendation (as opposed to length of book, size of type, pictures)

RETELLING RATING SCALE

	none	low degree	moderate degree	high degree
1. Retelling includes information directly stated in the text.				
2. Retelling includes information inferred directly or indirectly from the text.				
3. Retelling includes story structure.				
4. Retelling indicates setting.				
5. Retelling indicates theme or problem to be solved.				
6. Retelling indicates resolution of problem.				
7. Retelling includes most major points or events.				
8. Retelling includes supporting details.				
9. Retelling includes appropriate sequence of events.				
10. Retelling includes major characters.				
11. Retelling is coherent.				
12. Retelling is complete.				
13. Retelling is organized.				

FIGURE 7.3 Retelling records are helpful in finding out what a reader understood

Writing Evaluations

Written expression includes both composition and transcription. *Composition* typically refers to activities such as organizing ideas, establishing purpose, considering audience, and generating original text. The writer also selects a genre—expository prose, fiction, poetry, drama. *Transcription* refers to the use of accepted conventions when transposing language into written form. Such conventions include punctuation, capitalization, spelling, and spatial conventions (such as paragraph indention, margins). Since written expression is not just the end product but also the process involved, the process of writing may include preplanning, drafting, revising, and editing. The act of evaluating the written expression abilities of learners can be as multidimensional as the evaluator chooses. The following are strategies for evaluating written language:

Written Expression Checklists

Checklists help the teacher determine which skills the student exhibits consistently and which skills are emerging. Checklists may include items such as ideation, sentence structure, vocabulary usage, spelling, capitalization, and syntax.

When gathering data on a student's written expression, it is a good idea to compare three student-generated samples of the same genre. One sample alone may present an atypical picture of the student's abilities (see Figure 7.4 for a sample checklist).

Fluency

Students who do not write much are often low-risk takers, or they have been overcorrected so often they find writing anything but pleasurable. Because these students may write minimally, the teacher may want to record fluency. A simple way to do this is to calculate average sentence length (ASL). First, count the number of individual words and the number of sentences written by the student. (If the student doesn't use punctuation, use your best guess.) Divide the number of words by the number of sentences. Cartwright (1968) found that the average sentence length for eight-year-olds without a disabling condition was eight words. He also reported that ASL increases by approximately one word per year through age thirteen. Similar quantitative analysis can indicate variety of words used and correctness of grammar (see Figure 7.5).

After completing student checklists, the teacher can combine all the information on one chart in order to look at the class as a whole. Such a chart can help the teacher determine if students need a focused conference or mini-lesson.

Running Record of Writing Growth

For a running record of students' writing growth, Harste, Short, and Burke (1988) suggest a form divided into three sections: mechanics, strategies, and insights. Observations are recorded in the appropriate section along with the date and a reference to the written piece. In the "mechanics" section, for example, notes might concern the use of complete sentences and of punctuation (especially if the student has learned something new, such as quotation marks). The "strategy" section can comment on such things as "looked in journal to find correct spelling of Halloween." The "insights" section is for learner or teacher "Ahas."

Taped Response

When they have completed a written piece, students can record on tape what they like about their piece, what was difficult, and perhaps what improvement they would like to make. Teachers can respond to the students's comments on the tape.

Spelling

Choose one or several pieces of writing that seem typical. Record the number of nonconventional (invented) and conventional spellings and calculate the percentages periodically throughout the year. A numerical analysis of progress toward conventional spelling is also possible.

Self-evaluation

Not only is it important for the teacher to evaluate the learning going on in the classroom, it is equally important for learners to evaluate themselves.

CHECKLIST OF WRITTEN EXPRESSIVE SKILLS

Name: _____ Date: _____ Age: ___ Evaluation No. _____

	consistent	inconsistent/ emerging	absent	N/A*	comments

I. CONTENT
- A. Ideas—There is/are:
  - 1. Main idea
  - 2. Relevant information
  - 3. Descriptive details
- B. Organization: There is/are:
  - 1. Title
  - 2. Appropriate introduction
  - 3. Appropriate sequence
  - 4. Appropriately sequenced paragraphs
  - 5. Appropriately sequenced sentences within paragraphs

II. STYLE
- A. Intent
  - 1. Purpose is apparent
  - 2. Audience is considered
- B. Word Choice
  - 1. Correct words used
  - 2. Precise words used
  - 3. Variety of words used
- C. Sentence Structure
  - 1. Sentences are complete
  - 2. Sentences are clear
  - 3. Length varies
  - 4. Type varies

III. TRANSCRIPTION
- A. Syntax
  - 1. Verb usage
    - a. Correct S-V agreement
    - b. Correct auxiliary verbs
    - c. Consistent tense
  - 2. Pronoun usage
    - a. Correct reference
    - b. Correct subject/object
  - 3. Correct adjective/adverb usage
  - 4. General uage
    - a. Correct plural usage
    - b. Standard English used
- B. Punctuation
  - 1. End punctuation
  - 2. Commas
  - 3. Apostrophes
- C. Capitalization
  - 1. First word
  - 2. Proper nouns
  - 3. I
  - 4. Titles
  - 5. First word in quotation
- D. Spelling
  - 1. Uses beginning sounds
  - 2. Uses letter names
  - 3. Spells phonetically
  - 4. Uses traditional spelling

*N/A—not applicable
Analysis of individual items under each category is optional.

FIGURE 7.4 Written expression checklists record levels of skill in sentence structure, spelling, vocabulary usage, and syntax

---

WRITTEN PRODUCTION ANALYSIS

I. FLUENCY: AVERAGE SENTENCE LENGTH (ASL)
   1. Number of words   _____
   2. Number of sentences _____
   Divide the number of words by the number of sentences.   ASL = _____

II. WORD VARIETY: TYPE-TOKEN RATIO (TTR)
   1. Number of different words (type) _____
   2. Total number of words (token)   _____
   Divide token by type.   TTR = _____

III.GRAMMATIC CORRECTNESS RATIO (GCR)
   1. Number of total words   _____
   2. Number of grammatical errors   _____
   Divide total words by grammatical errors.   GCR = _____

IV. SENTENCE TYPES
   1. Total number of sentences   _____   _____ %
   2. Number of fragments   _____   _____ %
   3. Number of run-ons   _____   _____ %
   4. Number of simple sentences   _____   _____ %
   5. Number of compound sentences _____   _____ %
   6. Number of complex sentences   _____   _____ %
   To get percentage, divide number of type by total number of sentences.

Fragment: Part of a sentence is set off as if it were a whole sentence; lacks subject, verb, or both (It sunny).
Run-on: Two or more main clauses are joined together without punctuation or conjunction between them (It rained it snowed).
Simple: Single independent clause (It was warm in January).
Compound: Two or more simple sentences joined by a coordinating conjunction or semicolon (January was mild, but February was extremely cold).
Complex: Contains one or more subordinate clause as well as one independent clause (When the rain came, the people rejoiced).

FIGURE 7.5   Written skills can be quantitively analyzed

Self-evaluation helps students take responsibility for what they are learning and can be especially beneficial for students who are passive learners.

Literacy Survey

Ask students to fill out a questionnaire on their perceptions of their own ability, of others' ability, and the importance of being literate. Suggested questions include:

- Do you think you can read well?
- Do you like to read?
- When did you learn to read?
- Is reading hard for you?
- Is reading easy for you?
- What's the hardest thing about reading?
- What's the easiest thing about reading?
- Who do you think is a good reader?
- Why do you think that person is a good reader?
- Do you think it is important to read well?
- Will you need to be able to read well when you grow up and get a job?

- Do you think it's okay to read for fun?
- Do you like to write?
- Are you a good writer?
- What makes a good writer?
- Is writing hard for you?
- Is writing easy for you?
- What is easy about writing?
- What is hard about writing?
- Do you know someone who is a good writer?
- What do you think makes a person a good writer?
- Is writing important to you?
- What kinds of writing do you do now when you're not in school?
- What kinds of writing will you need to do when you grow up?
- Do you think it's okay to write for fun?

Self-Evaluation Checklist

Create a checklist that includes specific items students can use in evaluating their performance. Tailor the checklist to the students' writing level and goals.

FIGURE 7.6 Self-evaluation checklists should be tailored to the student's writing level and goals

SELF-EVALUATION

	do this well	need work on this	very hard for me	no experience
Select a topic				
Plan				
First draft				
Organize ideas				
Introduction				
Use of details				
Conclusion				
Use of active words				
Use of descriptive words				
Revise				
Edit				
Spelling				
Punctuation				
Complete sentences				
Creative story				
Letter				
Memo				
Report				
Poetry				

Comments:

SELF EVALUATION

For _____ unit

HOW DO I RATE MYSELF?

4 = Excellent   3 = Good   2 = Fair   1 = Not very good

_____ I listened to instructions and discussions.

_____ I participated in discussions.

_____ I did my share of the work in my group.

_____ I completed the reading and writing assignments.

_____ I read independently.

I LEARNED

Important facts such as:

_____

_____

_____

New words such as:

_____

_____

_____

I would like to learn more about:

_____

_____

_____

HOW DO I RATE THIS UNIT?

What I liked best was_____

The teacher really helped when _____

I would like the teacher to _____

In the future I would like to _____

FIGURE 7.7   Use self-evaluation checklists after a theme unit or group project

If both students and teacher complete an analysis, they can compare their perceptions (see Figure 7.6).

Unit of Study Self-Evaluation

Another good time to get students' input about their own performance is after a theme unit or group project. Figure 7.7 is an example of a student's evaluation.

IN CLOSING

The way we use evaluation procedures is often reminiscent of the familiar tale, "The Blind Men and the Elephant." In this story, six blind men each try to describe an elephant according to the part of the elephant he has come in contact with. After falling against the elephant's side, one proclaims that the elephant is like a wall. The elephant's tusk reminds another of a spear, while a third, upon feeling the elephant's trunk, thinks the elephant is like a snake.

The elephant's knee reminds the fourth man of a tree, the ear reminds the fifth of a fan, and to the sixth, the elephant's tail seems like a rope.

> And so these men of Indostan
> Disputed loud and long,
> Each in his own opinion
> Exceeding stiff and strong,
> Though each was partly in the right,
> And all were in the wrong!

We would be wise to learn from the men of Indostan. We cannot describe a learner's progress accurately by taking only one perspective. To the greatest extent possible, we must strive to evaluate the whole child within the context where learning occurs and is applied.

Yetta Goodman (1989) states that ideally, evaluation is an examination of the change that occurs because of the dynamics of curriculum, teacher, and students. It is not something that happens only at grading time or when school districts take a week out of learning time to administer group achievement tests. Regardless of the allure of "black and white" answers, there are no absolutes. Evaluation of human behavior must be ongoing and it must be a process of revision, because humans are never static. Evaluation should thus be viewed not as a science but as an art. It is also very much like detective work. What if students don't achieve on schedule, according to a curriculum guide or a developmental checklist? As Harste, Woodward, and Burke (1984) point out, some students who have "failed" according to the rules of the system may have learned how to play it safe, and their performance may not reveal all they know. As clever detectives, we need to catch learners demonstrating their knowledge.

There are many books which are devoted to assessment procedures which work well with whole language philosophy. Some are listed below.

Anthony, R. J. 1991. *Evaluating Literacy: A Perspective for Change.* Portsmouth, NH: Heinemann.

Bouffler, C., ed. 1992. *Literacy Evaluation: Issues and Practices.* Portsmouth, NH: Heinemann.

Brown, H., and B. Cambourne. 1987. *Read and Retell.* Portsmouth, NH: Heinemann.

Clay, M. 1993. *An Observation Survey: Of Early Literacy Achievement.* Portsmouth, NH: Heinemann.

Drummond, M. J. 1994. *Learning To See: Assessment Through Observation.* York: ME: Stenhouse.

Eggleton, J. 1990. *Whole Language Evaluation.* Bothell, WA: Wright Group.

Goodman, K. S., Y. M. Goodman, and W. J. Hood, eds. 1989. *The Whole Language Evaluation Book.* Portsmouth, NH: Heinemann.

Goodman, Y. M., D. Watson, and C. Burke. 1987. *Reading Miscue Inventory: Alternative Procedures.* New York: Richard C. Owen.

Grace, C., and E. F. Shores. 1992. *The Portfolio and Its Use: Developmentally Appropriate Assessment of Young Children.* Little Rock, AR: Southern Association on Children Under Six.

Harp, B., ed. 1993. *Assessment and Evaluation in Whole Language Programs.* Norwood, MA: Christopher-Gordon.

Herman, J. L., P. R. Aschbacher, and L. Winters. 1992. *A Practical Guide to Alternative Assessment.* Alexandria, VA: Association for Supervision and Curriculum Development.

Kemp, M. 1987. *Watching Children Read and Write: Observational Records for Children with Special Needs.* Portsmouth, NH: Heinemann.

Perrone, V., ed. 1991. *Expanding Student Assessment.* Alexandria, VA: Association for Supervision and Curriculum Development.

How to Use Evaluation Data

The previous chapter dealt with significant issues in evaluation and gave examples of evaluation strategies that would be meaningful and relevant in the whole language classroom. The important point is that evaluation should reveal information about students' learning progress and about how to enhance learning in the classroom.

Collecting the data is a good part of the work, but something has to be done with the data. Somehow we need to make sense of all the information we have gathered. Portfolios have gained a lot of attention and respect because they provide a way to incorporate both quantitative and qualitative data that meets the demands of primary and secondary stakeholders.

DESIGNING PORTFOLIOS

Portfolios have long been used by artists, musicians, models, photographers, and writers to showcase representative work. Business professionals likewise use portfolios to demonstrate their skills. Learning portfolios serve a similar purpose for students, and they have become popular among teachers for several reasons. First, they provide a framework for bringing together pieces of evaluative information. Second, portfolios showcase students' progress from a multidimensional perspective: they show academic progress, but they also include artifacts reflecting a learner's attitude and ability to cooperate.

Content and Organization

The contents of a portfolio can vary. The following list offers some ideas about what it might contain:

- evaluations (tests, checklists, rating scales)
- a summary of teacher observations

- writing samples (drafts, final copies, "published" books)
- tapes of oral reading
- a list of books read
- a graph showing the number of books read or stories written
- journal entries
- written or oral responses to reading
- scientific observations (for example, of eggs hatching)
- reports of student investigations or research
- oral or written accounts of feelings about a particular event
- artwork
- tapes of musical work
- videotape of an oral or dramatic presentation
- products from group work
- student self-evaluations

A learning portfolio is not just a random collection of artifacts, however. As Jerry Johns (1991) states, portfolios are different from student folders; they are the "intentional effort of professionals to legitimize the important role that naturalistic on-going evaluation plays in literacy assessment." For this reason, the portfolio should be organized around a specific purpose. An obvious one for special education students is to highlight IEP goals in the evaluation process that takes place within special education and set forth a common ground of reference for all stakeholders.

Assessment personnel, school district representatives, and state and federal agencies (secondary stakeholders) want to know the amount of learner progress from a comparative standpoint, and their need is typically met through formal testing. As a result, however, they only receive information about what has been tested and miss out on other qualitative information that gives a fuller picture of a child's progress. It's almost like looking through binoculars: we may be able to zoom in and focus on one area, but unless we look at the whole setting, we can miss out on a lot of information.

Teachers, learners, and parents (primary stakeholders) have a different set of needs. Teachers want to know about a learner's interests, attitudes, individual learning strategies, developed skills, and emerging skills. This information is critical in meeting individual needs. Learners usually want to know what they are learning, why, and how they are doing. Unfortunately, some learners stop asking these questions because school has become a tedious chore and their evaluations are always the same—not good. Parents usually want to know about their child's progress, and what they can do to support learning at home. Sometimes teachers complain that parents are not interested, but parents, too, may have become disenchanted if all they hear is negative.

Amazingly, all these needs can be addressed through the portfolio. The portfolio can consist of some type of folder or notebook (a three-ring binder or folder with brads works well because both keep papers in place while they are being examined). I also suggest that it be divided into sections that contain, for example, beginning-of-the-year data, such as standardized assessment and informal assessment (if desired); annual goals and objectives; observation summaries; materials related to academic areas, such as reading, writing, math; personal attributes (attitudes, interests, social skills); work related to the arts;

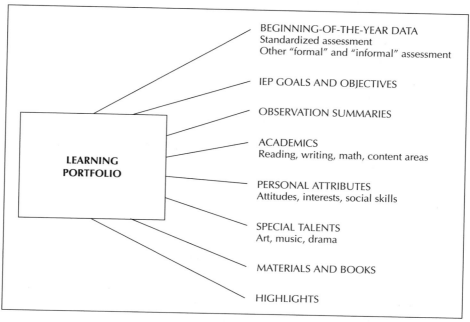

FIGURE 8.1   Identify learning objectives for the portfolio

materials and books used in the classroom; and a summary or highlights of portfolio (see Figure 8.1).

Student Ownership

Introducing the Idea

To implement a successful portfolio system in the classroom, students must be involved in the process from the very beginning. Students need to be made aware that a portfolio is not a collection of *everything* they do. They also need to be aware that an audience will look at their portfolio, which will include their parents and possibly other teachers and students. In other words, in their portfolio students exhibit what they have learned, learning in progress, and how they have applied their skills, strategies, and talents. The portfolio should showcase what the students can do without being compared to a "standard." To help her students have a better understanding of what their learning portfolio would represent, Pam Evans introduced the idea by having a parent, who also happened to be an artist, bring her portfolio to the class and explain how she selected the artwork she included.

Personalizing the Portfolio

Another strategy for getting students involved is to let them personalize the cover of the portfolio. Students often draw or cut pictures from magazines that represent their interests—cars, rock stars, movie stars, and sports icons. Some

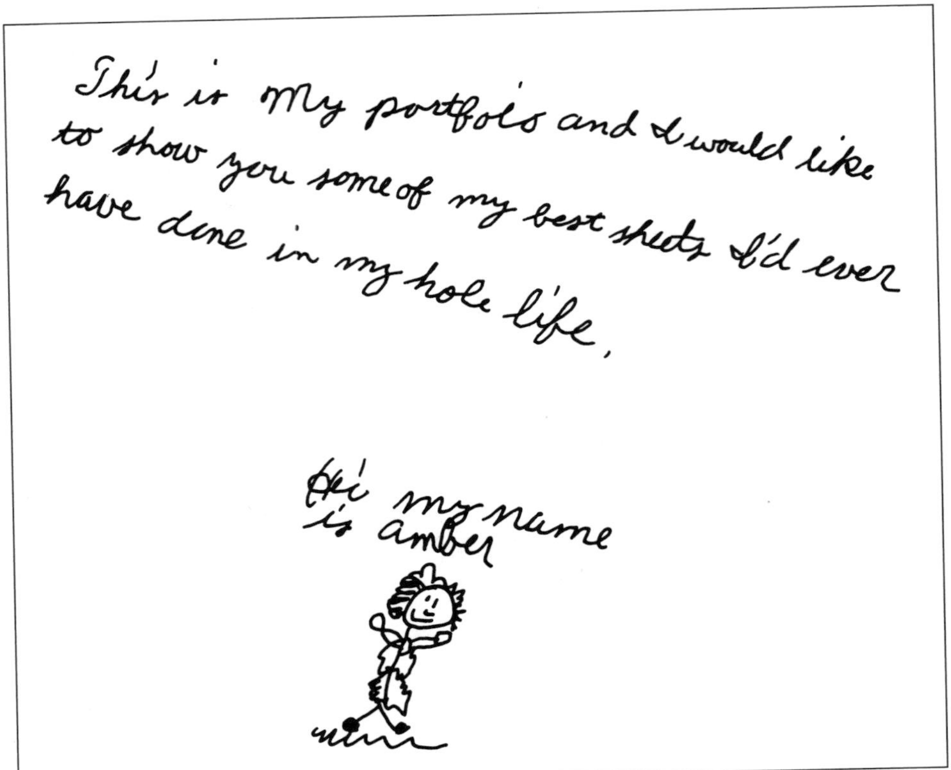

FIGURE 8.2 Students should personalized their portfolios

even like to make three-dimensional decorations. Students can also write an introduction (see Figure 8.2).

Making Selections

In order to be able to select representative work, students must save *everything*, so it is a good idea to have a "working" box or folder. Two important rules of thumb are

1. Don't let students take things home right away.
2. Record a date on *every* piece of work.

From time to time, teacher and student need to look through the working folder and make selections for the portfolio. The teacher should select a few pieces and the student should select a few. The teacher may want to focus on developed or emerging skills. Students may at first have a difficult time choosing. A few selection guidelines might be helpful. For example, choose one or two examples from several categories:

My best work
My favorite work
Challenging work

Something I started to figure out
Something new I learned
A solution I reached
Something I am proud of
Work in progress

With young learners and those that have difficulty making choices, Linda Lamme and Cecilia Hysmith (1991) suggest placing a limited number of samples in front of the child and asking which work the child considers the best and why.

After they have made their selections, both teacher and student must explain why they selected each piece. Before the initial portfolio conference, teachers can begin demonstrating self-evaluation. During an informal reading conference, for example, I have observed teachers saying something like, "I really like how you read to me today. Do you know why? . . . I noticed that you were using the 'skip it' strategy when you came to an unfamiliar word. You figured out every word except one through the context. Can you tell me what you like about your reading?" During writing conferences, these teachers use the same kind of demonstration: "I noticed in this piece you are using dialogue with quotations. I also notice that all of your sentences begin with a capital letter. What do you think is good about this piece?"

Initially, students may not have very sophisticated reasons for making their decisions: "I like the picture I drew," or "I made an *A* on this paper." After some practice, and through the teacher's example, students becomes more thoughtful. In the beginning stages, it is especially important not to send students the message that their reason is a poor one. The teacher may want to "plant" ideas by saying something like, "You made a good choice. I noticed on this paper you had periods at the end of all the sentences." Later, the teacher may ask questions, such as, "What are the strengths? What was difficult for you? Did you put a lot of effort into this work? What skills did you use?"

Each selected item should be accompanied by documentation, a brief description of the item, the reason for its selection, and who selected it. This can be accomplished with small forms (three-inch squares are a good size) that can be stapled or taped to the item or with a self-adhesive note (see Figure 8.3).

FIGURE 8.3 A small form attached to each portfolio selection tells who selected it and why

This is _____
_____
Selected by _____
because _____
_____
_____
_____
_____
_____

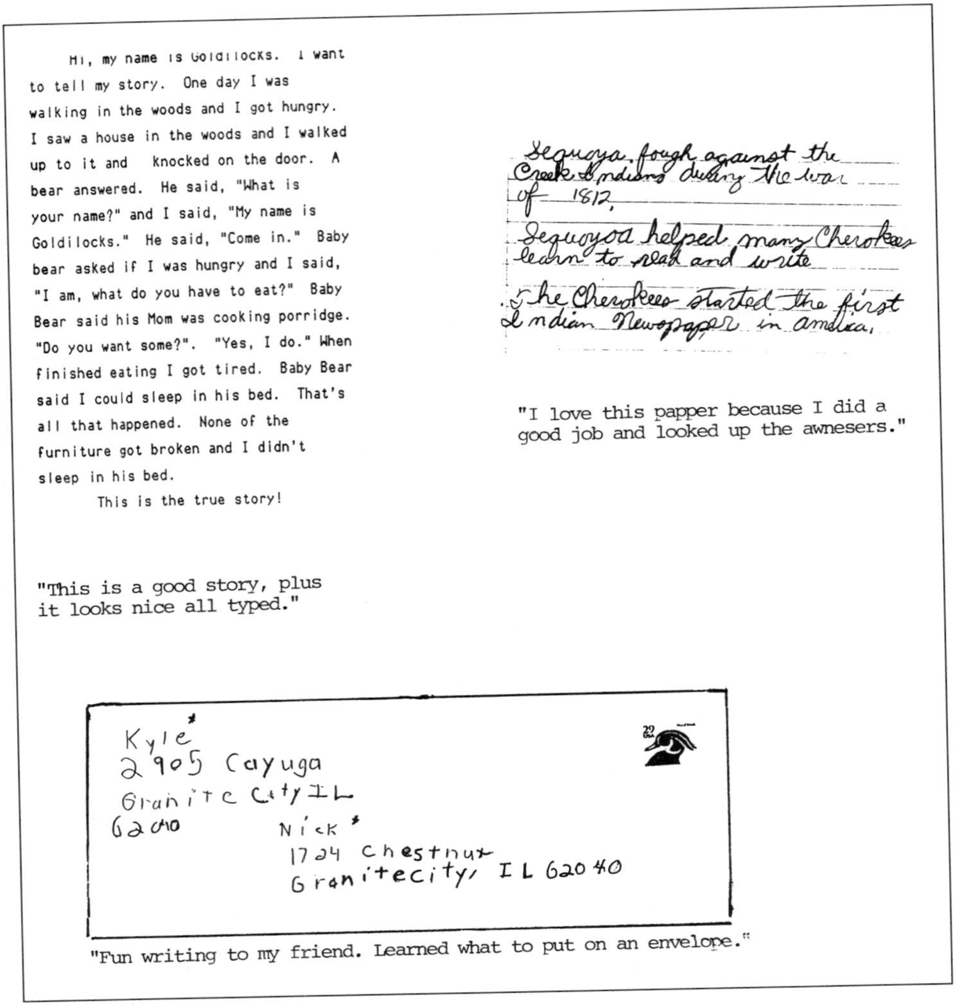

Hi, my name is Goldilocks. I want
to tell my story. One day I was
walking in the woods and I got hungry.
I saw a house in the woods and I walked
up to it and knocked on the door. A
bear answered. He said, "What is
your name?" and I said, "My name is
Goldilocks." He said, "Come in." Baby
bear asked if I was hungry and I said,
"I am, what do you have to eat?" Baby
Bear said his Mom was cooking porridge.
"Do you want some?". "Yes, I do." When
finished eating I got tired. Baby Bear
said I could sleep in his bed. That's
all that happened. None of the
furniture got broken and I didn't
sleep in his bed.
        This is the true story!

"This is a good story, plus
it looks nice all typed."

Sequoya fough against the
Creek Indians during the war
of 1812.

Sequoyoa helped many Cherokee
learn to read and write

The Cherokees started the first
Indian Newspaper in america.

"I love this papper because I did a
good job and looked up the awnesers."

Kyle
2905 Cayuga
Granite City IL
62040   Nick
            1724 Chestnut
            Granitecity, IL 62040

"Fun writing to my friend. Learned what to put on an envelope."

FIGURE 8.4   Student selected portfolio items

The collaboration between teacher and student helps establish learner pride and ownership. Not only does selecting work allow students to feel part of the evaluation process, it also increases their awareness of their strengths and abilities. In other words, it gives them a chance to call upon and practice *metacognition*. The learners become active participants rather than passive observers. Instead of "The teacher gave me a *C*," you might hear "Look what I did!" (see Figures 8.4 and 8.5 for examples).

Collaboration

Setting Goals

Portfolio conferences are a perfect time for students and teachers to collaborate on goals. With the teacher's help, students can discover how they are progressing toward their IEP goals and become aware of other areas in which they may be excelling. During an initial conference, the teacher may want to share a list of goals for academics, social skills, responsibility, self-management, vocational skills, self-esteem, physical wellness, and artistic endeavors. With the teacher's guidance the students can evaluate their progress and list areas that need improvement. Through collaboration, they can establish goals that may not be on the IEP.

Obviously this process is time-consuming, and teachers may want to do it only at the beginning and again at the end of the year, highlighting the goals by organizing the portfolio to reflect progress in these areas (see Figure 8.6). Any additional goals developed by the student should certainly be acknowledged at the IEP meeting and incorporated into the IEP. If at all possible, students should present their goals at the meeting themselves.

Parent Involvement

Parents need to know about learning portfolios and how they will be used. Teachers should decide how often the portfolio will be updated and sent

FIGURE 8.5 Teacher selected portfolio items

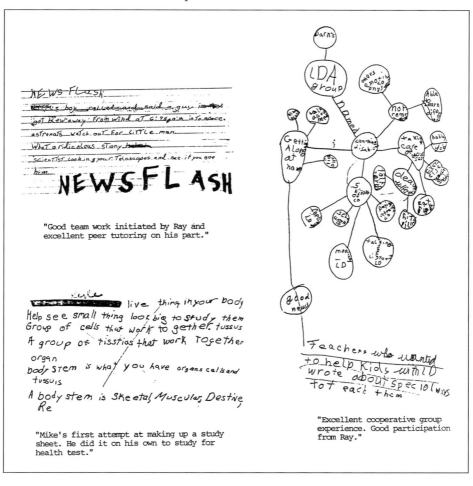

home—at the end of a grading period, quarterly, and so on. It is not necessary to make the portfolio additive; it may include only those items from a particular time period. Parents themselves can contribute to the portfolio by informing the teacher on what their child does at home, and artifacts from home might also be included. Another way to get this information is to develop a questionnaire for parents to refer to at home (Lamme and Hysmith 1991).

Communication

The portfolio is a wonderful vehicle for communication. It encourages teacher/ learner collaboration, parent/child collaboration, parent/teacher collaboration, and learner/parent/teacher collaboration. Both teacher and student can insert a summary page listing the student's accomplishments at the end (see Figure 8.7). Students may also want to summarize the highlights of their portfolio in a letter to their parents. This format often encourages parents to write back with words of encouragement.

Finally, the portfolio can encourage communication at the annual review of the IEP. Because evaluation has been ongoing throughout the year, reviewing and revising the IEP is less difficult. A portfolio, which represents the entire year, can document the student's learning and progress. It also puts formal test scores in a proper perspective: they become one piece of data among many in a whole picture. All participants in the meeting are made aware of the goals and objectives the child has actually accomplished. The IEP meetings should no longer be a mystery to students or their parents. Students should be invited to present their portfolios and participate actively in planning their educational destiny, and parents and teachers are invited to share their responses. When this occurs, the IEP meeting results in more responsive evaluation: stakeholders are recognized and asked to share meaningful information (C. Keefe 1992, 1993).

FIGURE 8.6   A contents page at the beginning of the portfolio lists goals

TABLE OF CONTENTS	
Profile of student	1
Student objectives	4
SECTIONS	
Introduction	I
Reading work samples	II
Social Studies work samples	III
Writing samples	IV
Math work samples	V
Working on being on time	VI
Learning about feelings	VII
Asking questions	VIII
Learning to introduce yourself	IX
Giving compliments	X
Making conversation	XI

ACCOMPLISHMENTS

I LEARNED

_____
_____
_____
_____

I READ

_____
_____
_____
_____

I WROTE

_____
_____
_____
_____

FIGURE 8.7 A page for listing accomplishments should be included in the portfolio

For learners with special needs, portfolios are a positive evaluation system. They also illustrate the legitimate use of naturalistic evaluation, which recognizes the markers of growth exhibited in daily work, and deemphasize formal test data.

By design, portfolios allow learners to become involved in the evaluation process. Because all children can and do learn, portfolios give teachers "permission" to be creative in documenting what they know about a child's progress rather than simply relying on test scores.

WRITING INDIVIDUAL EDUCATION PROGRAMS

Writers of an Individual Education Program (IEP) are typically instructed to express objectives in observable, measurable terms. Since they are making a projection—what the student will learn during the next academic year—objectives sometimes read like this: "When shown 20 consonant-vowel-consonant 'short a' words, the student will be able to read each word within two seconds with 80 percent accuracy." (Keefe 1993). Often these objectives are directly related to the standardized tests, criterion-referenced tests, mastery tests, and so on used by the district to measure progress.

The IEP is supposed to serve as an instructional guide, but there have been studies that call this claim into question (Dudley-Marling 1985; Lynch and Beare 1990; Margolis and Truesdell 1987; Smith 1990). These studies indicate that the objectives stated in IEPs may not be relevant to the student's needs and thus may not be the focus of instruction. A possible reason for the mismatch between IEP objectives and instruction is that the assessment measures used to develop goals and document progress do not reflect either authentic learning tasks or students' actual achievement. Teachers know this, and they go about using real classroom data to develop their curriculum.

Given all the alternatives discussed in Chapter 7, it is possible to write an IEP more responsive to learner needs. Current levels of performance, for example, do not have to be written in standardized test scores or mastery levels. Here are some alternatives:

Oral Language
The learner will

1. improve oral comprehension skills:
   a. be able to complete tasks successfully when given oral directions.
   b. be able to draw pictures to depict the sequence of events after hearing a story.
   c. restate directions or other information received orally.
   d. be able to summarize the main idea of a story.

2. improve narrative skills:
   a. participate in show-and-tell once a week.
   b. be able to retell a story orally, including the five elements of the story, as documented by a retelling rating scale.
   c. share ideas in a cooperative group.

3. improve pragmatic skills:
   a. use appropriate conversational skills (e.g., initiating a conversation, turn-taking, maintaining a topic)
   b. obtain information via the telephone
   c. successfully take leadership roles (e.g., class messenger, class monitor, group discussion leader)

The teacher will observe and document in oral language areas.

Reading
The learner will

1. demonstrate a more positive attitude toward reading:
   a. increase the number of books read by choice; progress will be documented by graphing the number of books read.
   b. demonstrate a more positive attitude toward reading; documented by comparing beginning- and end-of-year reading interviews.

2. improve reading comprehension:
   a. be able to demonstrate use of syntactic and semantic cues by successfully completing blanks in a cloze reading passage written at the student's approximate reading level.

b. after reading a narrative written at the student's approximate reading level, student will retell the story and include the five elements of the story; improvement will be documented by a retelling rating scale.
c. demonstrate the use of comprehension strategies (activation of prior knowledge, prediction, semantic mapping); observed and documented by teacher.
d. go back and reread when text doesn't make sense; improvement will be documented by teacher and with running records.

3. increase reading fluency:

a. increase oral reading accuracy rate; improvement will be documented with running records.
b. use "skip it and list it" bookmark strategy (see Chapter 11); use of this strategy will be observed and documented by teacher.

Writing

The learner will

1. be able to communicate in writing to various audiences by writing letters to:

a. obtain information.
b. communicate with a friend or family member.
c. communicate appreciation.

Artifacts from the beginning of the year to the end will demonstrate progress.

2. improve fluency of written expression:

a. increase average sentence length.
b. increase number of published pieces.
c. write in journal every day.

3. increase writing skills:

a. improve transcription skills. Improvement will be documented by analysis of writing throughout year using written expression checklist.
b. increase use of conventional spelling, as documented by writing samples throughout year.
c. demonstrate editing skills by checking sentence structure and proofreading for spelling, punctuation, and other conventions as documented by teacher and comparison of rough and final writing drafts.

IEPs can be designed for holistic instruction and they can be designed to meet the requirements of the law. The key to writing valid IEPs is the evaluation procedures used. By fitting evaluation to the curriculum, appropriate IEP goals and objectives can be identified.

ABOUT GRADING

Most teachers find grading a tedious chore, especially if it requires assigning a value to work that cannot be categorized as right or wrong. Some elementary and special education teachers are lucky in that they are allowed to write narratives about each child's individual growth. Unfortunately, however, grading policies are firmly in place in many school districts.

Here are a few ideas about grading:

- Make collaborative contracts with students. Set reasonable goals for individual student progress during the grading period. Obviously, a special education class includes such a variety of abilities, it is impossible to use the same criteria for grading everyone. The contract can articulate what level of work will rate an *A, B, C.* (See Chapter 7 for checklists and rating scales.) Grading criteria can also include effort, attitude, independence, and responsibility.
- It is not necessary to put a grade on everything.
- In order to let students get a feel for the process, allow them to "grade" a piece of their own work and explain why they gave it that grade. In other words, help students understand what is acceptable and what is not.
- Grading should reflect your instructional goals and the individualized goals of each student. When grades are mandatory, try to develop criteria and standards to meet these goals in advance. It is doubtful that you will come up with perfect criteria the first time, so don't be afraid to adjust as necessary.

IN CLOSING

Evaluation can be a positive process when it is organized and used in ways that encourage instruction and learning. It is not something that is done during a specified time period but a continuous process that draws on a variety of sources. Positive evaluation recognizes all learning progress. In addition, appropriate evaluation aids goal setting and monitors progress toward those goals. Curriculum should not be designed to enhance scores or outcomes. The evaluation procedure should be one that provides information about progress in the areas the curriculum has targeted.

Evaluation and grading are not synonymous: evaluation gathers data about progress, while grading assigns a value to a student's performance. If grades must be assigned, learners should be made aware of expectations.

Making Reading Whole

Reading is more than "R-r-run S-p-ot R-r-run." When children are identified as having learning problems, more than likely there is documented
"evidence" showing that they experienced difficulty in learning to read,
or they have already been labeled "nonreaders." Their reading instruction has
probably been "individualized" to remediate various deficit areas. Most remedial programs share a common philosophy: reading is primarily an audio/visual
process. Countless practice drills ask learners to identify and duplicate geomet-
ric shapes, match letters to sounds, and sound out both nonsense and real
words.

Kenneth Goodman (1968) and Frank Smith (1971) have made us aware,
however, that reading is a psycholinguistic process primarily, not a visual
process. Fluent readers probably don't think too much about what they do
when they read, yet they engage in common strategies. They select the most
useful cues and then, based on their background knowledge, *predict* what the
text will say. In other words, they do not read every word as a single unit. Their
eyes quickly scan the sequence of words and focus on the important, meaningful words. While they are *sampling* and *predicting* they are also *monitoring* their reading—were the predictions correct? Did that make sense? If not,
they back up, check it out, and possibly self-correct. If they encounter difficulty comprehending, they continue on, hoping that more information will
clarify the author's message, and they will be able to decode or comprehend
or both.

Many students learn phonics as their primary strategy for decoding words.
But some have great difficulty "sounding out" words, while others may be able
to "sound out" the words but fail to comprehend them because they are
concentrating on sounds rather than meaning. These readers do not learn that
decoding and comprehension are aided by using prior knowledge, predicting,
and self-monitoring. If children are having difficulty "sounding out" words, it
only makes sense to use this strategy sparingly. Instead, they need to learn how
to connect what they know to the printed words, how to predict, and how to
monitor. Unfortunately, it is not uncommon to drill these students on sound-

ing out or identification of sight words until they have lost sight of the fact that reading is the interpretation of a writer's written words.

At a university reading clinic, I observed Clark, an eleven-year-old boy with learning disabilities in a tutoring session. His only reading strategy was to attempt to sound out every syllable. It was painful to watch. The tutor started the session by reinforcing the boy's notion that reading is a visual process.

Tutor: Have you been practicing your flash cards?
Clark: Not really—we've been on vacation.
Tutor: Let's work on our "m" and "p" words from last week.

As the tutor held up the flashcards, Clark laboriously tried to sound out each word. For *pat,* for example, he said "ppp-aa-t." For *peg* he first said, "pig," then changed it to "pug," and finally to "peg." In each of these attempts he knew he had said the wrong word because the tutor continued to hold up the card, and so he continued guessing until the tutor set the card down on the table.

Don Keefe, the clinic supervisor, brought in a predictable Big Book, *My First Bike* (Keefe 1986). The text begins:

My parents bought me my first bike. I could not wait to ride it. My parents told me to get on and try it out. The first time I tried to ride my bike, I fell off and skinned my knee. I started to cry, but I didn't. Mom said, "It's OK. You can do it. Get back on. Try again." The second time I tried to ride my bike, I ran into a bush. I started to cry, but I didn't. Dad said, "It's OK. You can do it. Get back on. Try again."

The book continues through four more attempts by a little girl to ride the bike until finally she succeeds. The pictures illustrate what happens during each attempt. Don chose this book because he guessed that Clark would be able to relate to learning to ride a bike. First, he helped Clark establish his prior knowledge.

Don: Read the title of this book.
Clark: *My First Bike.*
Don: What happened the first time you tried to ride a bike?
Clark: I fell down.
Don: Do you think the girl in this story will fall down?
Clark: Maybe.

Clark read the first two pages and had some difficulty with the word *try* but eventually got it.

Don: How did you figure out the word "try"?
Clark: I knew "tear" wasn't right.
Don: What do you think will happen?
Clark: She'll probably fall over.
Don: That's a good guess. Let's read and find out.

Clark read the next page slowly but with success. He started to say "hand" for "knee" but settled on "knee."

Don: Why did you change the word to "knee"?
Clark: Because I knew it wasn't "hand" because it doesn't start with "hand."

Don: You're really using your brain! What do you think will happen next? Look at the picture.
Clark: She might run into a tree.

Clark read the next page.

Don: I noticed you read "bush." Why didn't you say "tree"?
Clark: Because it didn't start with a *t*.

Don continued to ask Clark to predict what would happen, and without being told, Clark looked at the pictures for clues in making his predictions. Later, as he was reading, Clark came to the word *neighbor* and was stumped. Don instructed Clark to skip the word and continue.

Don: Tell me what happened in the story.
Clark: A dog ran at her and made her fall off.
Don: That's right. How did you know what happened? You skipped that big word.
Clark: Well, I knew all the other words.
Don: So when you read this page, it made sense to you even though you didn't know that big word.
Clark: Yeah, I guess so.

Next, Clark attempted to read the passage, "The fifth time I tried to ride my bike, it wobbled and wobbled and wobbled until I fell off." When Clark came to the word *wobbled,* he couldn't figure it out.

Don: What word would make sense here?
Clark: "Moved" or maybe "bumped."
Don: Those are good guesses—they make sense. Do they start with the same letter?
Clark: No.
Don: So, you know the word is not "moved" or "bumped" but it's probably a word sort of like "moved" or "bumped."
Clark: Yeah, probably.

Probing Clark about the word *wobbled* was actually a quick and informal reading assessment. Don learned that Clark's syntactic and semantic cueing systems were intact. Even though Clark had difficulty with the word "wobbled," he said that "moved" or "bumped" would make sense. It was evident that he was using syntax cues because he chose verbs and that he was using semantic cues because he chose words indicating actions that would cause the little girl to fall off the bike.

As Clark continued reading, he still went slowly, but he was beginning to read whole words rather than breaking each word into individual sounds. Without being told to, he skipped words he couldn't figure out. His body posture changed: he was visibly more at ease, his shoulders relaxed, and I could see him scanning the pages looking at the pictures and seeming to try to make sense of what he was reading. Through Don's demonstrations and guidance, Clark was starting to make connections: he was using prior knowledge; he was making predictions and monitoring his reading; and he was learning that reading can make sense even if some words are at first too difficult to figure out. Using these simple strategies, Clark found reading easier, although he still had a long way to go—after all, he'd had five or six years of "sounding out" practice and only a few minutes of practice making sense out of reading.

BACKGROUND KNOWLEDGE

Being able to connect what we are reading to something familiar makes reading easier. Everyone has encountered reading material that was too difficult to understand because of technical terms or inadequate background knowledge. A friend of mine who was an economist often gave me books about economics for my birthday. I would dutifully try to read the books, but I simply could not comprehend them, which made me feel stupid. When he asked me about a certain book, I would say, "Oh, it was very interesting." Or, if he would talk about a particular part, I would smile and nod my head in agreement. Finally, it occurred to me that I shouldn't feel stupid. I simply didn't have the necessary background information, and I suppose I didn't really have the desire to acquire it.

Learners often face the same dilemma. They may be required to read a novel or text about an unfamiliar subject they know nothing about. Our challenge is to supply the background knowledge and experience.

For a period of time I observed a class of nine-, ten- and eleven-year-old children with moderate mental retardation. A student teacher had been placed in this class, and I was her university supervisor. Most of these children had not been exposed to many life experiences other than their immediate home environment and a few class field trips. In addition, they had not been read to very often. When the student teacher decided to introduce an animal unit, she discovered that the children knew very little about animals other than dogs, cats, birds, and a few farm animals such as horses, cows, and chickens. She began reading them books about zoo animals, but the interest they showed was, at most, adequate. After she took them to the zoo, however, they could hardly sit still while she would read books about lions, tigers, and monkeys. They wanted to touch the pictures and talk about every animal they had seen at the zoo. Whenever possible, they took the books off the shelf and looked through them independently. They also began drawing pictures of the animals and labeling the pictures with the correct names.

Providing background experience is just as crucial for older learners. In one junior high resource class, some of the eighth-grade students were included in the eighth-grade science class. A unit of study on nutrition was initiated, and all students were expected to pass a unit test in two weeks. The students told their resource teacher that they were really "bummed out" because there was no way they could pass the test. They had checked out the information in the chapter and it was full of long words and charts with lots of numbers. The teacher scanned the chapter and realized that tutoring them on the text material would not be very beneficial. However, she felt that the nutrition information was important and decided to implement a nutritional unit during the resource hour. Not all of the resource students were in the science class, but she thought they could all benefit.

She started by having each student write down what they had eaten for lunch that day. She then made a list on chart paper. The foods reported included pizza, hamburger, chocolate cake, chocolate candy bar, soda, and milk. She then had the students use one of the charts in the nutrition chapter to find information about the amount of calories, fat, carbohydrates, and vitamins in each of these items. They discovered they had a large intake of calories and fat. During the next several days the students continued their investigation of the foods they ate at home, in the cafeteria, and from vending machines. They began bringing in articles from magazines and used their science book as a reference to answer specific questions. The teacher also invited guest speakers, including a dermatologist and a college athlete, to talk about the importance of good nutrition.

During the second week, the teacher set aside several days to explore food. She brought in a variety of fruits and vegetables, along with interesting recipes. As students prepared different dishes, they discussed the importance of washing the fruits and vegetables and their nutritional value. At the end of the unit, the teacher did another survey to determine what the students were eating. The list now included some vegetables and fruits and less cake, candy, and soda. The teacher was delighted by the shift in eating habits, and the students in the eighth-grade science class were ecstatic because they all made a *B* or *C* on their nutrition exam.

INTEREST AND PURPOSE

Resource teachers have an especially challenging job because they have no control over the curriculum in general education classes. Their job is to provide their students the support that enables them to survive in these classes. The junior high resource teacher had two choices: help her students "get through" the science chapter and tutor them for the exam or provide experiences to make the information meaningful to them. Because she opted for the second approach, the students "got through" the textbook chapter while using the book as a resource to find out what they wanted to know.

Helping students learn to read and become life-long readers goes beyond teaching them skills, and even strategies. Readers read because they are interested in what they are reading or because they have a purpose. Unfortunately, many students with learning difficulties never realize that reading can be a pleasurable as well as an enlightening experience. Sadly, many of them view reading as torture, to be endured while they are in school.

Some teachers do help learners establish positive attitudes toward reading, and sometimes it's not the "showy" activities that make a difference. Mary was a second year teacher, but it was her first year in this building, and she had been assigned to be a resource teacher and inclusion support personnel. The psychological reports she received described quite a diverse group of youngsters, with reading disabilities, communication disorders, autistic tendencies, mental retardation, and behavioral disorders. The special education teacher for the primary-aged students tried to be helpful by giving her a "run-down" on the three students she'd had in her class the previous year: Two of them were no problem and could read on about a second-grade level, but Billy was a different story. He was practically a nonreader and had a very negative attitude.

Mary was overwhelmed and confused. According to the reports, her students' reading levels ranged from preprimer to third grade. Should she put them in different reading groups? What kind of materials should she use? She had been supplied with a stack of workbooks. She finally decided there was nothing she could do until she met her students in person. She devised a very simple plan. The first day of school she simply asked her students what their interests were. First, she had them make a list of the things they liked to do. If they couldn't write it, they could draw a picture. Later, they discussed TV shows and movies they enjoyed. By the end of the day she felt as though she knew enough about their interests to start collecting reading material. She ordered some trade books with her budget of $275. It would be a month or so before she received them, so in the meantime she collected books from both the school and public library, and spent several evenings pouring over discontinued and discarded basals searching for interesting stories on a variety of reading levels. She cut the stories out and bound each one separately in vinyl wallpaper covers. Within a few days she had a nice selection of books. She spread the collection out on a long table and gave a "book talk," briefly describing each selection. During their resource time, every child found a book, even several, to read. This was the beginning of her reading program.

As it turned out, Billy was not a nonreader. Several books were about horses, and he grabbed them before anyone else could get them. When he had finished those, he asked for more books about horses. His father was a horse trainer at the race track, and Billy knew just about everything there was to know about horses. He wrote several information books about horses and horse racing during the year and became the in-residence horse expert not only for the class but for the whole school as well.

Bert Hampton's high school special education students learned the joy of reading through comic books. Although not a new idea, it was new to Bert's students. The idea occurred to Bert after he listened to a tirade in the teacher's lounge on the lack of appreciation of good literature. An English teacher had just confiscated four comic books from her students. Later, Bert noticed comic books intermingled with "real" books in students' desks. He fondly remembered his own favorite comic book characters and decided to purchase class sets of a variety of comic books. With a great deal of ceremony, he presented them to his class. After the initial shock had worn off, his students began reading—really reading. The comics then became the basis for oral and written retellings, debates over current affairs and over moral issues presented in the stories, vocabulary development, and creative writing. Students also initiated research projects—Who conceived Superman? Who was the first X-Man? What comics did our parents read?

Marianne Doll, another high school special education teacher, strives to make reading important to her students through creating meaningful messages. She conducts a weekly contest to see who can guess the answer to a puzzle; written clues are posted on the wall and all guesses must be submitted in writing. In addition, she leaves personal messages on the chalkboard: "Willie came in first at last night's track meet in the high jump. He jumped five feet, two inches. Incredible!" or "Anyone who has clothing in my closet needs to take it home by Friday, or I'll send it to lost and found." Not only do the students read the messages, but they actually search for them and discuss them among themselves. Teachers who use message boards to encourage authentic reading and writing notice an increase in writing fluency. But they also notice that students shift from just writing notes to their friends to expressing opinions about relevant topics, such as school issues, the environment, and the use of drugs.

In her primary classroom Lyn Hart gathers her students, who are identified as mentally retarded, around a round table every morning to talk about the newspaper. She tells them that she and her husband read the newspaper every morning and shows them the various sections: "My husband likes to read about sports so he reads that section first. Look, there's a picture of Todd Zeile and Mark Whiten. Have any of you ever been to a Cardinals baseball game? [Several say yes.] The headline above the picture says, 'Expos Top Cards, Trail by 5.' What does that mean?"

Tony raises his hand and explains, "The Cards is the St. Louis Cardinals and the Expos is the name of the other baseball team. I think maybe they are from Chicago or someplace like that. I think maybe the Cardinals got beat."

Every morning, through demonstrations like these, Lyn helps her children become familiar with the newspaper and the kinds of information it offers. Often they each take a separate section and make their own discoveries, which they share with the rest of the class. After the morning talk, the newspaper is shelved in the class library, where students can look at it during their free time.

Other teachers find that cooking is an excellent way to demonstrate reading for a purpose. Barb Kinsella has a cooking corner in her classroom where she displays all kinds of labeled measuring tools. On the wall there is a detachable laminated poster that says "Recipe of the Week." Each week Barb writes down a simple recipe with a washable marker. On Friday she gives each student an individual copy of the same recipe to use while they prepare that week's special dish. From garage sales and inexpensive stores she has collected enough measuring cups and spoons so that students each have a personal set. First she reads the whole recipe out loud as the students follow along. Next they discuss the ingredients they will need. Then Barb reads the recipe again and demonstrates how to prepare the dish. After the demonstration, the students prepare the same dish individually or with a partner.

Sometimes older students need to practice reading with material that is repetitive and predictable, but stories like these may seem juvenile and insulting. Many teachers have had good luck enlisting the aid of younger students as an audience, thus establishing a reason for reading the "baby" books. For example, Jean Brunk, a high school special education teacher, knew that many of her students would benefit a great deal from shared reading of predictable stories. In order to make this activity meaningful, she discussed "adopting" a kindergarten class, and the students responded favorably. First, Jean demonstrated how to do a shared reading with young children. Her students knew that soon they would be doing this, so they watched very carefully. When the students had observed several demonstrations, they chose a book and practiced reading it as they would to the children. When they felt ready, individual students visited the kindergarten class as guest readers. This activity has proved to be beneficial for their reading but it is also a great boost to their egos because the kindergarten children and their teacher give the visiting reader lots of positive reinforcement.

IN CLOSING

It is important that teachers evaluate their role as learning supporters. Learning experiences will include reading, and as they develop worthwhile learning experiences, they need to ask a few key questions:

- Are learners allowed to use all the cueing systems?
- Is there an effort to connect background knowledge to new experiences?
- Is background knowledge provided when necessary?
- Is reading made purposeful and meaningful to individual learners?

Finding a Voice: Writing

When I work with veteran special education teachers, they almost always agree that reading and writing are the primary focus of their curriculum. However, when I ask them which is more important, I detect their discomfort. They're wondering if there is a right or a wrong answer. But I'm not really looking for a specific answer; I'm curious to know if they view one as more important than the other. Sometimes a brave soul will respond that she doesn't feel either one is necessarily more important; however, she spends more time on reading. Other teachers then concur, their basic reason being their own perceived lack of expertise in the area of writing. Perhaps that is why "formula writing" has become so popular with teachers. Formula writing refers to programs that reduce expository writing to a specific *number* and specific *kinds* of sentences (for example, topic or detail), and how they are placed in the paragraph.

During a discussion of writing, I asked these teachers to brainstorm all the different kinds of writing they do or have ever done. Here is their list:

directions
report
business letter
personal letter
postcard
mini-biography for an application to graduate school
research paper
captions for photographs
notes to husband/children
lists
observations
notes to self
letter of complaint
journal/diary
test items

invitations
thank-you note
flyer
interview

When they seemed to have run out of examples of their own writing, I asked them to brainstorm about some of the different kinds of writing they read but which we had not listed. This time, they added

advertisements
graffiti
books: fiction, informational, reference
articles: magazine, newspaper, professional
song lyrics
poetry
pamphlets, brochures
catalogs

Next, we grouped these different genres into categories and came up with six:

1. Entertain

   - articles
   - novels
   - poetry
   - song lyrics
   - graffiti

2. Inform

   - articles
   - flyers/pamphlets/brochures
   - directions
   - reports
   - research paper
   - notes to family members
   - business letters
   - informational/reference books

3. Share Feelings

   - personal letters
   - diary/journal
   - postcards
   - thank-you notes
   - letters of complaint

4. Persuade

   - advertisements
   - flyers/pamphlets/brochures
   - mini-biography for application
   - graffiti
   - catalog

5. Request Information

- test items
- business letter
- interview

6. Remind/Record

- lists
- personal notes
- minutes
- research notes
- captions
- observations

This exercise helped them see that they write much more than they realize.

We next talked about their approach to writing, and their reflections were similar to what researchers in the field call the "writing process." The writing process is a recursive act of planning and preparation, drafting, revising, editing, and, sometimes, what is referred to as "publishing" (Graves 1978, 1983; New Zealand Ministry of Education 1992). During the planning and preparation stage, also known as prewriting, the writer generates thoughts and ideas, identifies intentions, and begins basic organization. During the drafting stage the writer translates those thoughts and ideas into written form. This stage is complex because the writer must make decisions about word choice and sentence structure and along with the cognitive aspect there is the mechanical aspect of handwriting or keyboarding. Revision is the writer's effort to communicate more clearly by adding or deleting information, reorganizing sentences, and choosing words that more accurately express the writer's meaning. When a writer has done his or her best, it is time for final editing. The writer checks spelling, punctuation, and grammar before "going public" with the piece: publishing or sharing the piece in some fashion so that others can read and respond to it.

These stages, of course, are far from discrete, which is why the writing process is considered recursive. Writers move in and out of the various stages as they work on their pieces. It is not unusual, for example, for a writer to revise or even edit a bit while composing the first draft. (Sometimes a first draft may be the only draft.) Of course, not all writing is intended to be read by an audience other than ourselves; we do not take some pieces to the sharing or publishing stage (for example, lists, notes, personal writing), and we do little or no revising or editing.

I DON'T KNOW WHAT TO WRITE

When asked to write, learners who have a negative attitude toward writing may react in less than subtle ways, groaning and complaining; expressing displeasure nonverbally; avoidance behaviors (such as sharpening all their pencils); staring down at the paper, head in hand, for the entire period; or quickly writing a minimum number of sentences.

Teachers can ease the process for their students in several ways. First, as Cambourne (1988) has pointed out, the learner must perceive the task as doable and become engaged with it. To some learners, writing may seem anything but doable: they may have poor handwriting because of poor hand-eye coordination; they may have difficulty spelling words; or they may feel they have nothing to write about. In order to help learners perceive writing as doable, some teachers have discovered that free writing and group writing activities can be powerful jump starters. Writing activities such as "The Creature in My Backyard" and "A Day in the Life of Popcorn" (described in Chapter 11) take the writers through prewriting, drafting, and some revising. These demonstrations help students conquer the fear of writing and view writing as fun.

It is also important that teachers understand the need for plenty of time. Writers need time to germinate ideas (Graves 1983), and it is important for a block of time to be set aside for prewriting activities such as group brainstorming about a topic, field trips, drawing or sketching, dramatic activities, observing, sensory experiences, charting, outlining, discussing writing patterns in fiction or poetry, interviewing, research, and mapping. There are many books with wonderful ideas for encouraging student writing. Some of my favorite include *Creating Classrooms for Authors: The Reading-Writing Connection* (Harste, Short, and Burke 1988), *Living Between the Lines* (Calkins 1991) and *A Fresh Look at Writing* (Graves 1994).

Authentic writing is not an exercise; it has a specific purpose and addresses a specific audience. Letter writing is one effective way to encourage students who are reluctant to write. Christine Fresen uses the book *Free Stuff for Kids*, published by Meadowbrook Press, as a catalyst for writing. The book lists businesses that offer free and inexpensive items, along with their addresses. Christine's students really enjoy writing letters and postcards because they love getting mail. This activity has also had a useful carryover in other academic areas: one student, who needed to do a report on a state for a social studies project, on his own found addresses in this book where he could write for information about New Jersey.

Integrating purposeful writing throughout the curriculum helps learners understand the value of writing. Barb Kinsella asks her young students to keep a science notebook in which they record their experiments and observations. Their entries may consist of drawings, dictated observations, or their own written sentences, depending on their ability level.

Linda Joyce, a high school resource teacher for students with learning disabilities, uses writing as a vehicle for student self-assessment and instructional assessment in math via a math journal. Several times a week she gives them a journal prompt, such as the following:

Adam and Aaron each had a job and worked for five days. Copy the charts below in your journal.

Adam's Earnings		Aaron's Earnings	
Day	Amount	Day	Amount
Mon.	$5.00	Mon.	$5.00
Tues.	$7.00	Tues.	$5.00
Wed.	$4.00	Wed.	$5.00
Thurs.	$2.00	Thurs.	$5.00
Fri.	$10.00	Fri.	$10.00

Adam's earnings		Aaron's earnings	
day	amt	day	amt.
mon.	$5	mon.	$5
Tues.	$7	Tues.	$5
Wed.	$4	wed.	$5
Thurs.	$2	Thurs.	$5
Fri.	$10	Fri.	$5

① You would add it.

② yes you can figure the earnings the same way.

③ Add means to put all the numbers Together and find the Total. Adding is Better in Some ways Adding is easyer. multiplication is harden't your not good at it.

FIGURE 10.1   Journal responses help clarify a student's understanding of concepts

What is the easiest way to figure out how much money Aaron earned? Can you figure out Adam's earning the same way? Why or why not? Write a paragraph comparing the process of addition and the process of multiplication.

From their journal entries (see the example in Figure 10.1) Linda can determine if the students know the appropriate application of addition and of multiplication. These journal responses clarify for Linda and her students what they understand and what they are having difficulty with.

Teachers whose students are multiage learners with diverse abilities have found that creating a student newspaper or magazine is a good way to get everyone involved in a meaningful writing project. Students can choose to work on school news, reports on sports events, creative writing pieces, and interviews with people on topics of interest (one student, for example, interviewed his dad about Vietnam).

For one of my university graduate classes, I asked my students to find a way to integrate more meaningful reading and writing into their curriculum. One teacher felt this would be a very difficult assignment for her because she taught content-equivalent classes for health, math, and reading. After quite a bit of discussion, this teacher, who'd had some newspaper experience, reluctantly decided to initiate a project to develop a student magazine. Since she felt that she had to incorporate the subjects they were studying, she asked students to brainstorm ideas related to their class subject. The students took this opportunity to focus on topics that were relevant to them and to their peers, who were their target audience. The health students developed articles about nutrition and exercise; one student interviewed a dermatologist about how to have healthy skin. Some of the math students worked on sports statistics. Other features included a "Dear Cindy" advice column and a horoscope column.

The teacher really did not believe that this would be a worthwhile project or that it would engage the students. She introduced the project only because of her participation in the graduate class and my strong encouragement. I was sure it would be a success, and from my perspective it was. The students put together an interesting magazine, which other students in the school read, and in doing so obviously used their reading, writing, and research skills. When I asked this teacher if she would do another issue, however, without hesitating, she said, "No, it was too much work." As we talked, she revealed why it had been so much work: she had edited and typed all the articles herself and done the magazine layout. She had taken responsibility for making sure it was done "right." She wasn't yet at the point of trusting the students and letting them have ownership of either the process or the product. The students' projects became her projects, and yes, she did do a tremendous amount of work. Thus, from her perspective, the project was not successful.

Margarita Cotton introduced the writing process to her junior high resource class through friendly letter writing. First they discussed the idea of writing to a friend and the notion that someone they knew would be reading their letter. During this time, her students wrote to many different people, and she noticed that their writing style was different depending on who it was and how well they knew the person. They were not very concerned about spelling and punctuation, for example, when they wrote letters to their close friends.

In order to take their letter writing to a higher level, Margarita asked them if they had ever disagreed with anyone or reacted negatively to a procedure. The discussion prompted Margarita to invite them to write a letter to express an opinion. The students continued the conversation among themselves and eventually focused on a procedure the school principal followed: when the principal called the classes to come to the auditorium for an assembly, he would call students by grade level and then at the end, he would call the special education classes. Margarita's students were very upset about this and felt that it was unnecessary to single out the special education classes. They felt that they should go to the auditorium when their grade level was called.

The students decided to write a letter to the principal to express their feelings about this procedure. Because the letter was important and would have a very important audience—the principal—they wanted it to be "perfect." They decided that their best option was for the group to work together on one letter. To actually write the letter, they chose the person who had the best handwriting and was also a good speller. Each student made a contribution to the letter's contents. One girl even remembered the exact dates of the assemblies.

During this writing project, Margarita watched her students move through the various writing stages in a natural evolution. During the planning stage they discussed at length what they should include. The drafting stage involved contributions from each student. Revision was interwoven with the drafting stage as individual students commented on important points and suggested particular words. When they had completed the draft, they reread it and made further changes. They also checked spelling, capitalization, and punctuation. When the final draft was ready, they checked it again. Finally, they asked Margarita to read their letter and check for any spelling or punctuation errors they might have missed. When they were satisfied with it, they put it in an envelope and sent it to the principal. Their letter was now published—it was on its way to its audience.

The principal was astonished. He had never considered the negative effect of his assembly procedure. He apologized in person to the class and asked if they had other complaints. As a matter of fact, they did have other opinions to express and lots of questions to ask. As a result, the principal changed several procedures so that special education students were no longer singled out. This powerful letter is now framed and hangs over his desk.

Margarita was also astonished by this experience. She discovered that when her students had a meaningful purpose and an authentic audience for their writing, they found a voice and their "learning disabilities" disappeared. The learners shared a common goal, which they were able to accomplish. Perhaps most important, they saw that their voice made a difference.

JOURNAL WRITING

Journal writing has been common in classrooms for quite some time. It encourages learners to explore with their writing, to express their thoughts and feelings and take risks in applying what they are learning about written language.

From Margaret Glass's class of six-, seven-, and eight-year-olds, we collected journal samples written between September and May. The children, categorized as mentally retarded or learning disabled, had writing abilities ranging from scribbling to writing complete sentences with capitalization and punctuation. For students whose writing skills were in the beginning stages, their samples documented rapid growth. At the beginning of the school year their journal entries were scribbles and drawings, but by the end of the year they were writing sentences (see Figure 10.2). Entries between the beginning of the year and the end of the year included random letters, drawings with labels, words and lists copied from books and charts, and words they were learning to spell, especially color words, days of the week, and the names of classmates.

Students with more advanced writing skills wrote about the events in their lives and experimented with the conventions of print.
Sample journal entries:

- I like my horse. It is brown.
- I count find my shoes yesterday.
- I had a dream. It was about an earthquake
- I smelled a big rat in my cloet [closet].

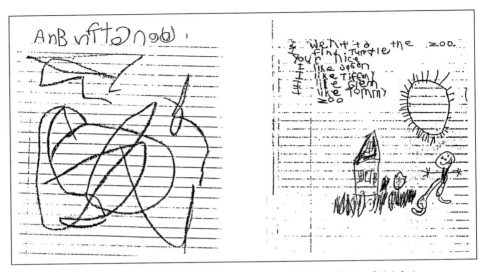

FIGURE 10.2   Brandy's journal entry in August (left), and April (right)

- I'm going to my grandmother's house. I love her. I like her games she gave me flowers.
- Today I'm go to McDonald. I'm eat french fries and Hambrgrs.
- I got to new VCRs. I got my TV back. It is big.
- I like Valentine hrts.
- I Lrnd how to SPEL Wrds

The writing these learners did in their journals during "choice" time had a different quality than their compositions during their organized writing time. During the organized writing time, Margaret guided them through the writing stages, conducted mini-lessons, and talked about what writers do. In their "formal" writing their handwriting was usually neater, they were more concerned about spelling, and they tended to include more detail. Figure 10.3 shows a formal writing sample done by the same student at approximately the same time as the April journal entry in Figure 10.2. The formal writing sample shows more variety in vocabulary and sentence structure, and this same observation held true for all the children.

During journal writing time, children could either experiment or practice what they knew. During formal writing time, the teacher employed the principles of L. S. Vygotsky (1978). Vygotsky, a Soviet psychologist who died in 1934, believed that language stimulates conceptual growth, and that conceptual growth is dependent on interaction with objects in the environment and with adults and older children. He set forth the idea of the "zone of proximal development"—the distance between a child's actual level of development and the level at which a child can function with assistance from an adult or a more able child.

This idea has had a significant impact on education. It reminds us that we must start where the learner is rather than fit the learner into a predetermined curriculum with group expectations. It has also caused us to think about how the opportunity to interact and receive support from those more knowledgeable and skilled boosts learning. Instruction is therefore most effective when students are challenged to stretch toward their next level of learning. Instruc-

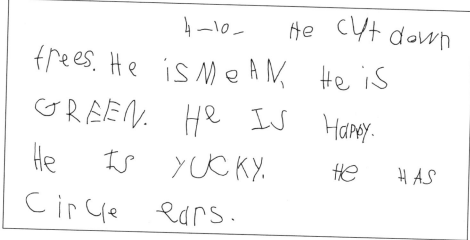

FIGURE 10.3   Another April entry in Brandy's journal shows a formal writing sample

tion is not effective if it is aimed below or above the proximal level (Sumner 1993).

For older students journals offer a place to express their personal thoughts and feelings. Many teachers report that the more they engage in dialogue with students, the more students write. (The major reported drawback is that sometimes teachers become overwhelmed by the amount of correspondence that results.) Often students reveal more of themselves through this informal format. Perhaps they feel it is a safer environment than a face-to-face conversation. I would, however, caution teachers about confidentiality of the journals. Students may reveal information that is meant only for the teacher, and of course, such insights can help the teacher understand how to nurture and foster the student's growth. On the other hand, students may reveal abuse or suicidal feelings that should be investigated further, since the safety of the student must come first.

CONFERENCES

A conference format is a very effective way to individualize writing instruction. After a first draft, revising and editing can be the most arduous part of writing. When novice writers finally get something onto paper, they usually aren't in the mood to change it. Assuming that their writing has an audience, however, and that it is a meaningful project they want to be good, they will need to consider revision and editing. Whatever genre the learner is exploring, writing conferences can be a nonthreatening way to help in clarifying and expanding. An editing conference is the logical time for mini-lessons in capitalization, punctuation, and grammar. What follows are suggestions for conferences adapted from Calkins (1984) and Graves (1983).

General Suggestions

- Do not be judgmental.
- Do not attend too much to specifics.

- Avoid too much praise.
- Show appropriate respect and appreciation for the writing effort.

General Questions to Ask

- How's your piece coming along?
- Are you having any difficulties?
- What's the most important point?
- What do you want the reader to know?

Eliciting More Detail

- Can you describe the place you're writing about? I can't picture it.
- You write that the dog is cute. What makes the dog cute?
- You write that you were very sad. If I were in the room with you how would I know you were sad? How would your face look? How would you walk?

Expanding

- What else do you know about this topic?
- If kids from another town read this, what questions would they have? Try to answer these questions.
- Read each line of the story and tell me more about it.
- Can you draw a picture? Act it out?

Not Coherent

- Is there more than one story here?
- Are there extra details that don't belong?
- Does the title fit the story?

Sequencing

- Let's list in order what happened in the story. Could the events be in a different order?
- Try cutting the story into separate sentences and putting them in a different order.

In addition to teacher-learner conferences, peer conferences can also be an effective arena for learning. For the most part students enjoy peer conferences, although they may not know what they should look for. To provide guidance, questionnaires for revision and editing are helpful. A revision questionnaire, for example, might ask:

What are the strengths of this piece?
What did you learn from reading this?
What part didn't make sense?
Are their details that should be added?
Were there any "tired" words that should be changed?
Are there any short, choppy sentences that could be combined?
Does the beginning get your attention. Is there a conclusion?

Through individual conferences, the teacher may discover the need for a small group or whole class mini-lesson. Although there may not be enough time to meet with each learner every day, it is definitely worthwhile to schedule a time for conferences as often as possible.

ABOUT SPELLING . . .

For years, interest in the written language of students with disabilities has rarely extended beyond handwriting and spelling. In fact, I suspect that many students have been referred or even labeled learning disabled because of their poor handwriting and "bizarre" spelling. For them, curriculum has been no more than drill on forming letters correctly and spelling words in isolation, without much thought to composing authentic texts. This seems a little absurd, since handwriting and spelling are skills applied during the act of composing. If students do no composing, then handwriting and spelling are of little use.

Spelling is Developmental

I often hear teachers remark that students "can't spell." Just as we question the notion "can't read," I think we should examine "can't spell." While it is true that some students in both special education and general education classes may not know how to spell every word they write correctly, their spelling often demonstrates a basic understanding of the conventional rules of sound-symbol relationships in the English language.

As research has revealed, spelling is not simply the act of memorizing sequences of letters; it is a developmental process (Beers and Henderson 1977; Gentry 1977, 1982; Henderson and Beers 1980; Read 1975). Richard Gentry (1982) applied a developmental spelling classification system to Glenda Bissex's (1980) case study of her son, Paul, and identified five developmental stages in learning to spell. His analysis is important. It shows that children who are exposed to written language and given opportunities to experiment with writing go through an evolutional process as they begin to understand the mechanical complexities of how oral language is transcribed in a written form that all speakers can understand.

The five stages Gentry identified include:

1. *Precommunicative:* alphabetic symbols to represent words but these demonstrate no letter-sound correspondence. They are attempting to communicate a message, but their attempts so far are not readable.

2. *Semiphonetic:* children use approximate representations of letter-sound correspondence and may represent whole words with one (or more) letter: the word *are* for example, may be represented by the letter *r*. In Bissex's study, at age five Paul wrote messages such as RUDF (Are you deaf), TLEFNMBER (telephone number), DP (dump), and OD (old). The letters he used to represent words are only a partial phonetic mapping of the word being spelled.

3. *Phonetic:* children represent every sound they hear. *Hambrgr* is a child's "invented" spelling for the word *hamburger* as he or she hears it. The child chooses letters based on their sound, without regard to conventional English spelling.

4. *Transitional:* children make a major move toward more conventional spelling when they include vowels in every syllable. They rely more on visual representation than sound representation. But because they are using a visual strategy, a word may contain all the necessary letters, but some may be reversed. The speller is not yet able to determine "what looks right."

5. *Correct:* children have established a knowledge base and develop finer discrimination with experience. "Correct spelling" is usually determined from an instructional level.

Gentry makes several important comments that teachers should keep in mind in evaluating spelling. First, developmental levels should be determined by spelling miscues, not by words spelled correctly. It is not unusual for spellers to have "automatic" spellings for certain words (cat, me), even at the precommunicative level. Second, the major cognitive changes necessary for spelling competency may be completed by the end of the transitional stage. Children develop further through frequent writing experiences and some formal instruction.

Conditions for Learning to Spell

The same conditions necessary for learning language are necessary for learning to spell (Cambourne 1988). Learners need to

- be immersed in a print-rich environment
- see demonstrations of the sound-symbol relationship
- be expected to learn
- make decisions about the words they learn to spell
- have time and opportunity to use and practice their developing knowledge of English orthography
- feel free to experiment with approximate spelling
- receive appropriate and constructive response in a non-threatening manner
- feel that spelling is doable and purposeful

Spelling is one of the skills needed for writing. It develops over time when nurtured in an appropriate environment where children have ample opportunity to practice. Here are seven suggestions for nurturing spelling skills:

1. Immerse learners in reading and writing. Through reading learners encounter correct spelling. By writing themselves, they apply and refine their spelling knowledge.

2. Make learners aware of resources for correct spelling. As part of the immersion process learners need easily accessible models spelled correctly. They should be made aware that it is *permissible* to refer to wall charts, books, dictionaries, and other resources at appropriate times. Show students how to use a spelling dictionary, a small book listing words in alphabetical order with no definitions. Encourage students to create word banks or personal dictionaries. A personal dictionary can be made by inserting blank paper in any kind of folder. Write a letter of the alphabet at the top of each page. When students ask for the correct spelling of a word, the teacher writes the word on the appropriate page. Students then refer to their personal dictionary for the spelling of that word. Below is a list of dictionaries that provide short lists of common words and space for students to add words.

> Hollway, J. 1989. *Writing Dictionary.* Scarborough, ONT: Ginn Publishing Canada. (May be ordered through Steck-Vaughn, Austin, TX.)
>
> Hurray, G. 1987. *A Spelling Dictionary for Beginning Writers.* Cambridge, MA: Educators Publishing Service.
>
> Sitton, R., and R. Forest. 1987. *The Quick-Word Handbook for Everyday Writers.* North Billerica, MA: Curriculum Associates.

In addition, teachers and students can create wall charts listing words related to content-area studies.

3. Encourage learners to take risks and try approximations. When children are drafting a piece of writing it is important that they get the main thoughts and ideas down on paper and not worry about correct spelling. Many learners are literally so "hung up" on spelling, they never get to focus on the composition aspect of their writing. It is difficult for them to write a complete thought when they are overly concerned about words they do not know how to spell correctly. It is not uncommon for these children and adolescents to write brief sentences using only simple words they know how to spell. They have probably already received the clear message that all words must be spelled correctly or they will be penalized (penalties may take the form of points taken off or writing out misspelled words five to ten times each).

4. Demonstrate temporary spelling. I do not advocate ignoring incorrect spelling. What I do advocate is untying some of the knots and relieving tension about writing by teaching students to use temporary spelling or placeholders when they are composing. If necessary, spelling can be corrected during the editing process.

Teacher: Sometimes when I'm writing I may not know how to spell a word, but I don't want to stop writing because I might forget my idea. I try to spell the word they way it sounds. For example, I want to write the sentence "Halloween is on Friday," but I'm not sure how to spell *Halloween.* First I say the word and listen for the first sound. What sound does Halloween begin with?

Students: H.

Teacher: What other sounds do you hear?

Students: H . . . L . . . W . . . N.

Teacher: Okay, I'll write, "HLWN is on Friday." Later, when I finish writing, I'll find out how to spell *Halloween*. Where can I find the correct spelling of *Halloween?*

In my own research I have observed that children with learning disabilities and mental retardation who used temporary spelling eventually learned to spell words they used often in their writing correctly.

5. *Forget weekly spelling lists.* Requiring learners to memorize a list of spelling words every week is ineffective. I was once asked to do an assessment of a twelve-year-old boy with learning disabilities to determine the "severity" of his spelling disability. His mother insisted that the boy should be exempt from written work: his spelling disability was so severe, his written work was noncommunicative. The professionals who worked with the boy felt that exempting him from writing would be a disservice to him because he would lose any opportunity to improve his writing skills. It would contribute to dependent behavior.

During my investigation I learned that the boy made an *A* on his weekly spelling tests and thus *A*'s in spelling on his report card. But this was misleading because his spelling grade did not reflect his ability to spell in a written context. When I asked him how he managed to do so well on his spelling tests, he said he memorized the words immediately before the test. Like many of us who have memorized information for a test, however, he forgot them as soon as the test was over.

Even more important, time spent studying, memorizing, reviewing, and being tested on isolated words on lists is time lost to real reading and writing in authentic and meaningful contexts. We learn to spell most directly by seeing words when we read and trying to visualize them when we write. Every activity that involves spelling in any way should be called "spelling" so that students (and parents) recognize that working on writing is working on spelling.

6. *Let the learner determine pace and direction.* Learners of the same age have a wide range of spelling abilities. One learner in the third grade might be at the "correct" spelling stage, while another learner in the same class might be emerging from the phonetic stage into the transitional stage. The specific course of development for an individual child is influenced by what he or she reads and chooses to write. Other influential factors include the child's interest in spelling, concern for correctness, level of visual awareness, and encouragement (Wilde 1990). Because of differences in development and other factors, instruction aimed at an entire group will not be appropriate for every individual learner. Spelling instruction based soley on a spelling textbook or workbook cannot respond to students individually. Cutting lists in half or selecting "words of the week" does not take individual differences into account. This type of instruction views the brain as an "empty storehouse" that is gradually filled with words and rules (Wilde 1990).

7. *Provide learners with usable strategies.* Some usable strategies have already been addressed. Here are a few:

- Show students how to use a spelling dictionary, a small book listing words in alphabetical order. No definitions are given.
- Have students make their own personal dictionary. Blank pages can be

stapled together with alphabetic dividers. Students write words they have difficulty with in the appropriate section.
- Demonstrate writing a word with alternative spellings to determine which spelling "looks right."
- Think about related words.
- Think about parts of words.
- Teach rules judiciously only when students are capable of using them and if they need them. Wheat (1932) determined that only four spelling rules are predictable enough to be worth learning: 1. when *ei* or *ie* should be used; 2. dropping silent *e* before a suffix; 3. changing *y* to *i*; and 4. doubling consonants before suffixes. Another handy rule is that the silent *w* occurs only before *r*, and silent *k* only before *n*.

Grading and Evaluation

I personally do not advocate giving a separate grade for spelling. However, some teachers do not have the luxury of choice, and sometimes parents demand a grade (spelling is important in our society). On this subject Sandra Wilde (1990) makes an excellent point: "Most spelling grades given in traditional programs probably reflect developmental level and natural ability more than anything else, which is equivalent to assigning grades based on yearly increase in height" (p. 287). The same can be said for standardized spelling tests.

To evaluate spelling progress some teachers use grade-level sight word lists. At the beginning of the year students are asked to spell the words on the chosen list but they are not given the list to study. Then, approximately every two months, students are again asked to spell the words from the same list. Over a period of a year, these spelling "tests" will demonstrate improvement in spelling through the immersion in print characteristic of a whole language classroom.

If teachers must give a grade for spelling, there are alternatives to spelling tests. Here are some ideas:

- Give a grade based on spelling accuracy in final writing drafts (taking developmental level into account), and students' use of available resources.
- Base grade on markers that show progress. A checklist of items can include

  risk taking (attempts to spell unknown words)
  use of resources for spelling
  spelling of words targeted in mini-lessons (such as dropping silent *e* before *ing*)
  proofreading (recognizes correctly spelled and misspelled words)

- If a spelling test is an absolute must, let students choose their own words. In addition, consider making the test voluntary and having it administered by a classmate or a student from an upper grade.

Grades and evaluation are not synonymous. Evaluation provides information about actual progress. Sandra Wilde (1989) outlines the four major principles of a research-based spelling evaluation model:

- Evaluate spelling on the basis of natural writing. Use stories, letters, reports, and so on to determine how learners use spelling as a tool for written communication.
- Evaluate spelling analytically, not according to whether it is "right" or "wrong." Be aware of such factors as developmental stage and dialect, which may influence phonetic spelling.
- Look at spelling in terms of strategies. What resources does the learner use? Does the learner experiment with spelling rules?
- Evaluate spelling as an informed professional rather than relying on a mechanical test.

READING AND WRITING CONNECTIONS

There is no question that reading opens up worlds that are far away or otherwise inaccessible to most of us. But how often do we consider that, as the learners in our classrooms become readers and writers, we are able to experience their joys and disappointments. As children sit in a sharing circle and listen to a peer's written piece, they learn about another person's thoughts and feelings. Sometimes it is comforting to know that someone else feels the same as we do. Sometimes it is a surprise that a classmate knows so much about horses or the ocean. (And, of course, teachers are susceptible to these little surprises as well.)

Some learners in our classroom may have such great challenges, they are not yet able to participate to a great extent in the magic of sharing through the written word. Yet, while their progress may be slow, their accomplishments are no less amazing, as in the case of Cornita. Cornita, a ten-year-old, is

FIGURE 10.4 Cornita expresses her own thoughts about an upcoming trip to the zoo

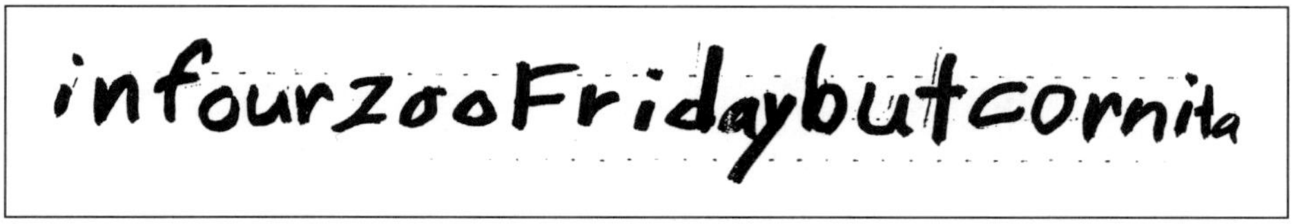

FIGURE 10.5 Unable to accompany her class to the zoo, Cornita writes her disappointment

identified as mentally retarded. Lyn Hart, her teacher, engages the students in a variety of literacy activities, which include journal writing. For the most part, Cornita's journal entries have been drawings or copied words. Only slowly did she begin writing words and thoughts independently. One day she wrote about the upcoming class trip to the zoo: "Is but zoo four Friday" (Figure 10.4). However, because she had gotten herself into trouble at school, she was not allowed to go on the field trip. While the rest of her class went to the zoo, Cornita stayed at school. At some point she wrote in her journal: "In four zoo Friday but Cornita" (see Figure 10.5). In her teacher's eyes, this was a major breakthrough. Cornita's two entries represented a huge accomplishment. The next week, Cornita had another breakthrough. The class had been reading and singing a song about Pterodactyls. It had the repeated phrase, "I'm small but I can fly." Later, as she was reading her library book Cornita recognized the word *fly*. Her eyes became tremendously big when she realized that she knew the word *fly*. Not only did she know *fly*, but she knew *kite* and many other words. "I can read this book!" she proclaimed to anyone and everyone that came into the room. Cornita was reading and writing on her own. She viewed herself as a reader and writer. Cornita will be able to open many new doors and invite others into her world. All she needs now is encouragement and opportunities to read and write.

Supporting Diverse Learners

Literacy development is a continuum stretching from novice to expert rather than a series of points of skill mastery. According to traditional school organization, learners in a specified grade should fall within the boundaries of "average" development. If any learners fall considerably outside this predetermined range, they are often pulled out for special help. The ideal teaching situation for decades has been a classroom of students with approximately the same reading, writing, and mathematics ability. If students are too low or too high academically, they are culled out so that teachers can devote their time to the majority without having to devote inordinate time to a few. This is known as the "relief philosophy." The flipside is that the "misfits" are taken out of the "homogeneous" classroom because they are failing or not receiving the attention they deserve. This is known as the "rescue philosophy."

CENTER OF THE CLASSROOM—CURRICULUM OR LEARNERS?

Teachers who work with children and adolescents with learning difficulties have always faced the challenge of meeting the needs of a very diverse group of learners. However, since schools are now deciding to include special learners in regular classrooms to a greater extent than ever before, all teachers are being called upon to become aware of differences and to support a variety of learners.

As classroom communities become more inclusive, teachers will need to reexamine how they approach teaching and how they organize the classroom. No longer can the curriculum be the "center of the universe," and scope and sequence charts navigate the paths of learning. Many learners simply don't fit—and can't be made to fit—into these neatly organized charts, which spell out progress. As a result, learners do not meet expectations; they are required to practice more; they may be pulled out for special help; or they may be retained. Take Max, for example. He is a seven-year-old who has the privilege of "doing first grade" again. There was some discussion about referring him for special education services, but after due deliberation by the first-grade teacher, the principal, and his parents, he could have "another chance" in first grade.

What happened to Max? Max came to school eager to learn and perceived himself as a learner. But his teacher didn't perceive him as a "good enough" learner. Although he could read many predictable books, the first-grade curriculum mandated mastery of certain phonics skills and sight words. Max couldn't make sense of the phonics worksheets, and sounding out words in isolation was beyond his ability. He was placed in the lowest reading group, one that rarely got to do "real" reading. It is ironic that the children who most needed to be engaged with reading were deprived of the opportunity for the sake of meaningless drills. At the end of the year Max had not progressed satisfactorily and was retained. This is a typical case in which meeting the standards of the curriculum was more important than meeting the learner's needs.

The case of Tamara is an example of a student's experience in two contrasting educational environments. Tamara, an eight-year-old, had been in a self-contained class for children with mild/moderate disabilities since she was six. Fortunately, her teacher designed the classroom learning environment around the learners, providing optimum conditions for literacy learning—immersion, demonstrations, and endless opportunities for learners to practice their emerging literacy. It was obvious that the teacher expected each student to learn, and students viewed themselves as readers and writers. Tamara progressed very well in reading. Her teacher mainstreamed her into the general education first-grade reading class, and she was able to keep up. Her special education teacher continued to provide her with appropriate supports so that she could develop strategies for interacting with printed text. By the end of the year she had finished the stories in the required first-grade basal series.

The next year, however, Tamara moved to another school, and the special education multidisciplinary team decided that Tamara would participate in the regular second-grade reading class. At the beginning of the year the second-grade teacher based her reading groups on whether students had progressed through the first-grade series. Those who had completed the series were put in the "High" reading group. Guess what? Tamara was placed in the high reading group because she had completed the series. As long as Tamara was reading stories and books she functioned fine; but, as might be imagined, her downfall was the workbook pages. She simply couldn't make sense of the abstract tasks required to complete the worksheets. Eventually, Tamara was moved to the lower reading group so she would have more time to do her workbook pages.

Tamara would probably have continued to progress in reading if the teacher had been aware of her "zone of proximal development" rather than focusing only on the dictates of the curriculum. As we saw in Chapter 10, the zone of proximal development is the distance between a child's actual development and the level at which the child can function with assistance (Vygotsky 1978). This notion is quite different from presenting something from the curriculum and requiring students to practice, or reteaching what they haven't learned yet. The key element is *interaction*. Teachers provide "doable" demonstrations based on learners' needs, and then learners try their hand. Teachers observe and listen, congratulating learners when they make tiny steps forward and acknowledging their close approximations. Finally, they provide learners with the assistance they need to boost their level of development.

If we want our students to become independent readers and writers and, eventually, independent learners, we need to support their independence by helping them develop personally useful skills and strategies. Some learners internalize literacy processes so quickly, it seems that they become fluent readers and writers almost without effort. Others, however, have great difficulty developing the skills and strategies they need to become fluent readers and writers. But drilling them on isolated skills is not beneficial, nor is putting interesting books in front of them and saying, "Go for it."

Both the reading process and the writing process are based on meaning making. They involve reconstructing someone else's meaning or constructing one's own meaning. Readers must figure out the author's intentions, and writers must consider how best to communicate what they want to say. These skills and strategies develop over time with the support of teacher demonstrations and through practice with real reading and writing. Learners *grow into literacy*. We should not assume they start out reading and writing as fluently as adults.

LITERACY DEVELOPMENT

The continuum of literacy development encompasses several stages:

Emerging Stage: Learners become aware of symbols and print in their environment. They develop an awareness of sound-symbol relationships, and they use their knowledge of social context to figure out how print works.

Expanding Stage: As their literacy expands, learners develop strategies for figuring out unfamiliar words. These might include asking themselves, "Does this make sense?" or "Is this word spelled like another word I know?" Gradually they become aware of textual conventions. They are also challenged to associate their knowledge of both print and content with what is written on the page. In other words, they integrate prior knowledge, word identification and comprehension strategies. During this stage readers learn about the structure of sentences and how structure affects meaning. As these processes begin to develop, however, readers tend to lose fluency.

Fluency Stage: As learners become more fluent readers and writers, they have more control over their thinking. They begin to plan how they will construct answers, make interpretations, and experiment with ideas. In addition, they select, organize, summarize, and synthesize information from various sources to justify and support a point of view. For further discussion, see Mooney (1991) and Walker (1992).

These stages are not bound by age or grade level. For example, many adolescent learners could actually be considered emergent readers. Although they have been "taught reading" for five, six, or seven years, the notion of what reading is about has not yet clicked. While the stages of literacy development are not absolute, they can perhaps give teachers a conceptual framework for

	emerging	expanding	fluency
Good Literature	•	•	•
Shared Reading	•	•	
Logo Books	•	•	
Taped Books and Stories	•		
Predicting	•		
Language Experiences Stories	•		
Invitations to Write	•	•	•
Print Copying	•		
Labeling	•		
Story Chunks	•		
Pattern Writing	•		
Predicting and Confirming	•	•	•
Free Writing	•	•	•
Journal Writing	•	•	
Chunking	•	•	•
List It and Skip It Bookmark	•		
Written Conversation		•	
Jumpstarts for Writing		•	
Story Frame		•	
Journalism Questions		•	
Semantic Mapping	•	•	•
K-W-L-S		•	•
Skimming and Scanning		•	•
Reader's Theater		•	•
Request		•	•
Buddy Reading		•	•
Reciprocal Teaching		•	•
Learning Logs		•	•
Literary Discussion		•	•
Literature Circles		•	•
Author's Chair		•	•
Activity Centers		•	•

TABLE 11.1 Demonstrations, Mini-lessons, and Strategies to Support Stages of Literacy Development

evaluating their students' literacy needs that will guide them in assisting literacy development.

By observing students as they read, using the evaluation techniques described in Chapter 7, and referring to stages of literacy development, teachers can achieve a fairly good sense of where students fall along the continuum. The following selected demonstrations and mini-lessons are effective with learners who are struggling with literacy development. Some of the strategies are a response to common roadblocks: teachers often comment, for example, that they have difficulty getting some students to use prediction. Others are concerned about students who read laboriously and without regard to meaning. These demonstrations and mini-lessons are not intended to be implemented in isolation but to be used as sources for support within the context of a particular learning event. It is always best to determine the learners' needs and then select strategies that match those needs.

BASIC DEMONSTRATIONS

Good Literature

Students in special education classes do not always have the opportunity to read good literature. Yet good writing allows learners to appreciate a good story and piques their interest to read more. The New Zealand Ministry of Education uses several criteria for piloting and selecting scripts for their *Ready to Read* series. These criteria are applicable to most reading material for the primary level, and they may also be useful in selecting material for older children as well. (See Mooney [1991].)

1. Does the story have charm, magic, impact, and long-lasting appeal?
2. Is the idea worthwhile?
3. Is the story's shape and structure appropriate? Is there an identifiable beginning, middle, and climax with acceptable resolution? What gaps must the reader fill in?
4. Is the language effective?
5. Is the story authentic?
6. Do the illustrations help the reader gain meaning from the text?
7. Is the format of the book appropriate?

There should be three levels of reading material available in the classroom:

- Stories/books that learners can read independently.
- Stories/books that are challenging but can be read with teacher support.
- Stories/books that the teacher reads to the students.

To create interest in a story or book, set the stage. Some teachers read part of a story or novel while students follow along and then ask students to read silently. As the story progresses there should be lots of discussion of the characters and the events. Reading aloud to children teaches them a great deal about reading: how to hold a book, turn pages, direct eyes left to right, find story clues in pictures, predict what will happen, and retell the events of the story. Most important, they learn that print on the page means words, and the written code begins to make sense. Reading aloud is not just for the young; older students enjoy the same benefits.

Picture Books

Picture books have long been used in the lower grades, but they have also proven beneficial to older learners. This is especially true for poor readers who are capable of discussion but do not have the attention span for longer books. Picture books can be challenging and help students gain the confidence they need to approach a longer book. In addition, they work well as part of a curriculum theme. The book not only becomes part of the learner's prior knowledge, it also serves as an excellent advanced organizer. Learners can also enjoy and appreciate picture books for their beautiful illustrations.

Choral Reading

It is not unusual for students with learning problems to be grouped together according to a label rather than according to their developmental level. One classroom may contain a range of ages and developmental levels. Engaging such diverse learners in a whole group activity is somewhat challenging. Choral reading is an activity that lends itself to such diversity. It can feature more challenging reading selections because the teacher or more capable readers can read the primary parts. For example, a reading selection can be divided so that more able readers are given the harder and longer parts and less able readers repeat the easier and shorter parts. Because this activity is done as a group, students have more support, feel less singled out and are more willing to take risks.

EMERGING LITERACY

Shared Reading

Teachers of young children like to use Big Books so everyone can see them. Don Holdaway, a New Zealand educator, introduced the idea of using Big Books to simulate the intimate environment of parents reading to their children. In the classroom, a group of children huddle close to the teacher and book, recreating that intimate environment. Books chosen for shared reading should use predictable phrases, repetition, or rhymes so that the children can quickly begin reading along with the teacher. It is important that the teacher point to the words as she reads to demonstrate voice-print match. The shared reading experience is an excellent way to encourage confidence in reading because children are able to read the book without assistance in a short time.

Logo Book

Have students look through advertisements in magazines and newspapers to find familiar logos for stores, candy, drinks, toys, and so on. Have students cut out and categorize the logos; for example, my favorite snacks, stores, or restaurants. Have students paste the logos on separate pages according to the category. These pages can be stapled together or put in a folder to make a logo book for students to read.

Taped Books and Stories

Record favorite stories and books on audiotapes so that developing readers can listen and follow along in a printed copy. Such assistance allows developing readers to feel in control: they can choose what they want to listen to and how often.

Predicting

Part of the process of understanding or constructing meaning from a text is being able to hypothesize about what we are reading. When young children are first learning to read, we ask them to guess what the story is about. We want them to get their "brains ahead of their eyes" so that the act of reading is more purposeful and meaning centered. Reading is more than saying one word after another. Predicting is a relatively simple task for most children, especially those whose home environment is literate. For some learners, however, predicting may not come easily. They may be low risk takers who are simply afraid of being wrong, or they do not know how to make guesses based on their own experience. Val Meyer and Don Keefe (1990) suggest the following activities to encourage predicting:

Wallet Predicting

Ask students to guess what is in a wallet or purse. Most students will have some success because they have often seen their parents and others take money out of their wallets. They probably also know that a driver's license and credit cards are usually kept in wallets. When students guess correctly, it is important to stress that they were able to do so because they used their prior knowledge. The teacher might ask, "How did you guess what was in my purse?" The students will probably indicate that their mother has money in her purse. The teacher responds, "You made a good guess because you thought about what your mother has in her purse."

Number Predicting

Prepare index cards with predictable patterns, such as 2, 4, _ , 8, 10, or a b _ d e _ g h.

Prepared-Story Predicting

Write a simple short story that features the learner as the main character and includes factual information about the learner. Have the learner read some of the story and then predict what will happen next.

Language Experience Stories

Language experience stories help learners to see the connections between oral and written language. The learner dictates a story, and the teacher writes it down on chart paper.

Dictating a story may be difficult for some learners; it is important to arrange activities they can later describe: for example, cooking, trips, a previously read story, or an interesting picture. When the learner has dictated the story, he or she then reads it out loud from the printed text with assistance from the teacher as necessary. The story can be read again and again.

For emergent readers and writers, language experience activities have several advantages. They demonstrate the relationship between the spoken and written word. Next, because the words are the learner's, the content is familiar and the learner is able to understand the print. Although students may not recognize all the words, they are more likely to take a chance and guess—correctly—because they know what it *should* say.

Invitations to Write

The teachers must believe that students can write, and they must provide frequent opportunities for them to freely express their ideas—in pictures, scribbling, random letters, and so on. In addition, it is essential that the teacher express an interest in the message the learner has communicated. Some teachers find it helpful to transcribe the child's message on a self-adhesive note that can be attached to or removed so that the original work is not altered.

Print Copying

Encourage students to copy words, phrases, sentences or whole stories from books. This activity helps them understand how letters go together to form words and begin noticing capitalization, punctuation, and other conventions. Children will often choose this activity during choice or free time, but it is best linked to a meaningful purpose such as writing a note home or a happy birthday message to a friend.

Labeling

Invite learners to make labels for objects and locations in the classroom, such as equipment, furniture, supplies, locations, Reading Corner and so on.

Story Chunks

If it appears that the student has memorized a language experience story or a predictable story but has not really connected with the printed words, copy the story in chunks onto cards and ask the student to read the cards in the order they appear in the story. For students who have difficulty, the teacher may ask helpful questions: "What did you say in the story after . . .?" (Walker 1992).

Pattern Writing

After reading a predictable book or story as a group or by themselves, students can try writing their own version using the pattern already established. For example, an excerpt from *What Do You Eat?* (Keefe 1986) reads:

> Bluebird, bluebird, what do you eat?
> I eat the worms that live in the ground.
> Black cow, black cow, what do you eat?
> I eat the grass that is easily found.

In their versions, students can change the names of the animals and the colors: "Yellow duck, yellow duck what do you eat? I eat the bugs that live on the ground."

Predicting and Confirming

To encourage readers to make predictions as they read, the teacher can give a demonstration:

> *Teacher:*   Look at the picture on the cover. What do you think this book is about?
> *Children:*   There's a cow and a bird and a barn. It's about a farm.
> *Teacher:*   This book is *What Do You Eat?* by Donald Keefe. Do you want to make another guess?
> *Children:*   Maybe it's about what farm animals eat?

The teacher writes the predictions on a piece of paper, on index cards, or on the chalkboard. Next, read the first few paragraphs or the first page to check predictions. If predictions are correct, students deserve compliments. If not, they can discuss why. The teacher should then demonstrate predicting what might happen in the next paragraph, page, or section and have students read to confirm the predictions. The teacher continues through the entire story in this manner, stopping at logical places for reader confirmation. On the written list, correct predictions should be checked off and incorrect ones crossed out (Meyer and Keefe 1990).

Free Writing

The purpose of free writing is to push reluctant writers to write without being overly critical of themselves. The free writing period is a specified length of time during which writers are instructed to write anything without stopping. Peter Elbow (1973) suggests that if writers can't think of anything, they should write, "I can't think of what to write" over and over or write the last word they've written over and over. Over a period of time, free writing often helps writers shift their attention from spelling and other conventions that can cause writing blocks.

If students have difficulty selecting topics, brainstorming beforehand might help. Special education teachers often report that free writing does indeed help reluctant writers. It gets their "juices" flowing and gives them an outlet for built-up emotion. It "frees" students who continually correct their work to take a few risks.

Journal Writing

Journals let students write about topics that interest them without worrying too much about spelling and other conventions. Journal entries are dated and kept in chronological order to show progress over time. Most learners keep diary-style journals in which they write about personal experiences, feelings, or any topic they choose. Some teachers give students sentence stems to get them started, but this should be done sparingly and eventually not at all. Sentence stems or starters take away the child's ownership, and the teacher's idea of a "clever" starter may not intrigue everyone. For example, "The worst day of my life was when . . ." may seem promising, but students may not want to think about the worst day of their lives. If it is necessary to nudge, present a variety of choices and let students select. In addition, be careful about imposing criteria for entry length. If there is a three-sentence minimum, some students will write only three sentences. To encourage students to write more, ask specific questions. It is also important to let the students know you value what they have written by offering specific comments: if a student writes about eating pizza, for example, you might respond with something like "I really like pizza, too—especially pepperoni."

Chunking

Less fluent readers often benefit from demonstrations in how to "chunk" words together. First, demonstrate ways in which reading is similar to speaking or thinking. When we speak or think to ourselves, the words we use are grouped or chunked together in phrases. In describing a bicycle, we might say, "the blue bicycle" as one complete thought unit. We would not say "the (pause) blue (pause) bicycle." Show how this principle works in reading by reading poems or short stories aloud. In addition discuss why the appropriate phrasing is important to meaning.

EXPANDING LITERACY DEVELOPMENT

As learners progress through school, they face texts that present more and more challenges, especially in content areas such as social studies and science. It is important to give struggling learners a few strategies to help them confront these challenges with more confidence. Although many learners manage to discover strategies on their own, those who are struggling may be "strategy deficient," they may not use appropriate strategies, or they may use strategies that are too simple. Several hypotheses have been proposed to explain why some learners are lacking in strategies for approaching texts or have an underdeveloped sense of how to use them. One possibility is neurological immaturity or damaged development of the brain centers required for coordination. Another possibility is the child's home environment: communication and instructional patterns at home may not allow children to solve problems or encourage them to assume responsibility for monitoring their own behavior. A third possibility is school failure: continued failure in school influences the teacher's expectations of the child and manner of communicating with the child.

The following techniques are useful in helping students develop their own individual strategies for comprehending, organizing, and storing information.

List It and Skip It Bookmark

Students may read laboriously and without fluency, and have difficulty with comprehension, because they have been taught to sound out every word. As a result, they lose an ongoing sense of the meaning of the text. They are "welded" to a phonics approach to reading. In the past the phonemic cueing system has been overused and the syntactic, semantic, and pragmatic systems have been underused. Readers with this problem need to realize that it is not necessary to know every word to understand the meaning. It is permissible to skip words and continue reading; often the unknown word becomes clear through context. A cloze activity can make this point. If a word in a sentence is covered up, a reader can usually guess what the word is through the context. But even if students understand the concept of figuring out words from context, convincing them to skip words they don't recognize immediately may be difficult. They may have had years of phonics drill and breaking away from sounding out unknown words may be scary.

Meyer and Keefe (1990) suggest a procedure that helps students unwind themselves.

Make bookmarks with "List It and Skip It" written at the top. If the bookmark is laminated it can be used over and over. Ask students to write any unfamiliar word they come across while they read on the bookmark. (An alternative is to use self-adhesive notes.) After they record the word, they should continue reading. When they have finished, ask them to cross out the words they "discovered" as they read further. Next, help them figure out the words they did not cross out by using context clues, the dictionary, or sounding-out strategies. Finally, discuss which words they think it would be important to know and invite them to write them down on an index card to file or in a notebook for future reference.

Written Conversation

In a written conversation (Burke 1985), students carry on a conversation with a partner through writing only—no talking. To illustrate the procedure the teacher should ask a student volunteer or teacher's assistant to participate in a written conversation on the chalkboard. For example:

> *Teacher:*   Hi, Sara. How are you today?
> *Sara:*   Fine. How are you?
> *Teacher:*   I'm sleepy. I stayed up late.
> *Sara:*   Why?
> *Teacher:*   I watched a movie.
> *Sara:*   What movie?
> *Teacher:*   I can't remember. What time did you go to bed?
> *Sara:*   9:30.

After students have observed this demonstration, ask them to find a partner and experiment. By writing on the same piece of paper, they can reread their whole conversation afterwards.

Jumpstarts for Writing

Teachers have discovered that involving students in low-stress group writing activities helps break down barriers to writing. The following activities work well with most learners.

Creature in My Backyard

1. Pass out unlined paper and instruct students to fold the paper in half horizontally, keeping the fold at the bottom.
2. Invite students to draw the head of a person, an animal, a space alien, or any creature they can imagine. The only requirement is that they place the creature's neck at the fold.
3. Instruct students to turn their paper over so that the fold is at the top.
4. Ask students to pass their paper to the person next to them and to repeat this a second time.
5. Instruct students to draw a body but without looking at the head on the other side of the paper. The body should be placed so that the shoulders will connect with the neck on the other side.
6. When they have finished, again ask students to pass the paper twice.
7. Everyone opens the paper they are now holding, looks at the "creature," and perhaps gives it a name.
8. Next, do a brainstorming activity. Have the students pretend they hear a loud noise in their backyard that causes them to look out the window, when they see this creature. Have them brainstorm about what kind of creature it is, where it came from, why it's there, and so on.
9. After the brainstorming activity, invite the students to write a version of "Creature in My Backyard."
10. When they have finished, have students share their stories with the entire class or with a small group.

A Day in the Life of Popcorn

1. Give each student popcorn or some other item of food and explain that together, they will be doing a sensory exploration.
2. Have students name the five senses—sight, smell, sound, touch, taste—and write these words across the chalkboard, on a chart, or on a transparency.
3. Have students observe the popcorn and think of all the words that describe how it looks. List these words under Sight. Next have students smell the popcorn, brainstorm words describing how it smells, and list these words under Smell. Continue this procedure to explore all the senses, listing words that describe how the popcorn feels, sounds (while eating), and tastes.
4. Review all the descriptive words on the list.
5. Next, give students a situation for a group story in which they incorporate some of these words. For example, they might pretend that the popcorn can walk and talk and then create a story about "a day in the life of a piece of popcorn." Write down all their suggestions and have students write one story as a large group or a small group, or individually.

Story Frame

The story frame exercise helps readers define which characters and events are important and aid their own writing. The teacher introduces a story by inviting children to predict what will happen. As the teacher reads aloud she stops to discuss the student's predictions and talk about characters, problems, and resolutions. When she has finished reading the story, the teacher discusses with the students who they think the most important character was and why. She charts their answers under the headings character, problem, solution. The teacher then asks if the characters in the story had a problem that needed to be solved (again recording answers). Finally, the teacher elicits a discussion about whether the problem or problems were solved and how. Students then write a summary of what they perceive as the most important events of the story.

Journalism Questions

Journalists are taught to answer six simple questions: who, what, when, where, why, and how. If students seemed to get bogged down in retelling an event or story or seem stumped about what to include in a written piece, demonstrate how answering these six questions will insure that they have included all the major elements of a story. To practice in an authentic context, have students report school or community news or conduct interviews for a class newspaper.

Semantic Mapping

Semantic mapping is a multipurpose process that aids students in assessing their own background experience and knowledge, connecting new concepts to information they already know, and generating research questions about a topic.

Write the target concept on the chalkboard and draw a circle around it. Next, have students brainstorm related words and ideas. As they do so, the teacher lists the words and ideas on the chalkboard. Then students try to formulate general categories into which the words and ideas fall (such as appearance, habitat, food, behavior). For example, if the topic was snakes, the list might look something like this:

long	lives in the ground
mean	lives in trees
dangerous	eats insects
slithers	black
eats small animals	have scales

The teacher then writes the categories around the targeted concept and draws a line connecting the concept to each category (see Figure 11.1). Students decide where their brainstormed ideas fit.

Discussion of categories inevitably leads to questions, and these should also be noted. As a postreading activity, students can check the accuracy of the "map" and add new information. Teachers may want students to copy the map and place it in their individual notebooks, since students frequently use these maps for study guides and even create their own maps independently. The maps also can be used to organize a research paper: each category (appearance, food) becomes the subject of a paragraph in the body of the paper.

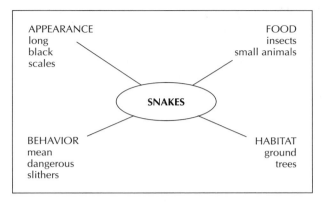

FIGURE 11.1   Semantic mapping connects concepts and information

K-W-L-S

Prior knowledge influences our interpretation of what we read and enhances our comprehension. All students have experience and background knowledge in a variety of areas, but some may not be aware that they can draw on their prior knowledge to make their reading more meaningful. K-W-L-S is an acronym for What I *K*now, What I *W*ant to Know, What I *L*earned and What I *S*till Need to Learn. A technique originally described by Donna Ogle (1986), it shows readers that they already know something about a subject, and that their knowledge can help them in understanding a text. This strategy can be used with individual learners or in a group setting and it works well with nonfiction selections at any grade level. (Originally there were three categories, the third being a combination of What I Learned and Still Need to Learn. Arne Sippola (1995) suggested separating the third category into two separate categories.)

1. K Step: What I Know. Accessing prior knowledge includes two phases: brainstorming and chunking. During the first phase, the teacher engages students in brainstorming to find out what they know and records responses in a list or a semantic map on the chalkboard, on chart paper, or on an overhead projector transparency. The teacher should be very specific. If students have decided to learn about the Pueblo Indians of the Southwest, the teacher should ask what they know about Pueblo Indians, not something as vague as "Have you ever been to New Mexico or Arizona?" If students do not have much information about Pueblo Indians, the question can be broadened to, "What do you know about Indians?" To help students clarify their thinking the teacher can ask such questions as, "Where did you learn that?"

During the second phase of "What Do You Know," students look at the information they have listed and decide whether some of the items can be chunked together in a general category (such as description, where they live).

2. W Step: What I Want to Know? As students brainstorm about what they know, they naturally think of questions. The teacher encourages this process by highlighting conflicting information or gaps in information. Questioning is a group activity, but it is a good idea to have students write down the questions they're particularly interested in before they begin reading. This establishes a purpose: each reader reads to answer his or her own questions.

3. L Step: What I Learned. After students have read the selection, discuss or have students write about what they learned and check their questions to see if they have been answered.

4. S Step: What I Still Need to Learn. Readers attend to any unanswered questions or items that need further investigation. At this stage, teachers may want to suggest further reading. Ogle suggests using a worksheet with columns at the top and a place to write identified categories at the bottom. The worksheets can be kept throughout the year to evaluate changes in a child's ability to access prior knowledge.

Skimming and Scanning

Less able readers may struggle with content area texts because of complex syntactic and semantic structure and dense information. "Getting through" a reading assignment may be an almost impossible task. Special education students in a mainstream class are expected to glean information from the text so special education teachers often highlight main ideas in the text for their students. This practice, however, tends to create dependency. Teaching students to skim and scan allows them to become self-sufficient readers and to access information quickly. *Skimming* is useful for identifying main ideas and themes. Give students practice in skimming by asking them to read a paragraph within a time limit and determine the main idea. Point out that the first and last sentences may reveal the main idea. Next, give students longer passages that have several paragraphs. Include selections with subheadings and demonstrate how headings give the reader a snapshot of the context.

Scanning is a way of finding specific information when we have neither the time nor the desire to read an entire chapter or article. Telephone books and newspapers make good practice material. Have students think of an item of information they need to locate in a phone book or newspaper. Show them how to look for key words to focus on the specific piece of information. Then demonstrate how to generalize the skill to textbooks.

Readers' Theater

Readers' Theater can include a dramatic reading of a play, a story, excerpts from a book, a poem, or some combination of these. The script is a symbol of Readers' Theatre and should be in an easy to handle notebook. The notebooks should be uniform in size and color (Coger and White 1967). Develop a script by dividing the reading into parts. Where necessary, a narrator can set the stage and supply important information. Students interpret characters through vocal intonation and perhaps a few small props. (There is no significant stage movement.) They do not necessarily memorize lines and sit on stools with a printed script propped on a music stand. Participants focus on what the author is trying to communicate. Often, as a natural consequence, students' oral reading becomes more fluent and expressive.

Request

"Request" is another technique that gives readers practice in connecting what they already know with what they are currently reading (Manzo 1969). It relies on role reversal—the student becomes the teacher, and the teacher plays the part of the student. The teacher introduces the story and asks students to read the whole story—or a portion of it—silently. When they finish, they take the role of teacher and ask questions about the story. The teacher responds by connecting what she already knows with the information in the text. The roles switch back so that the teacher can ask questions focusing on predictions or inferences.

Buddy Reading

Older, struggling readers often refuse to read books on their independent reading level because they consider them "baby" books. But if these students don't practice their reading, they will not make much progress. One solution is to give these readers a way to see themselves *as readers* by setting up a "buddy reading" program with kindergarten or first-grade students. This arrangement gives older readers a legitimate reason to practice reading "baby" books, and it enhances their confidence as readers because younger students are thrilled by the attention they receive (Samway, Whang, and Pippitt 1995).

Reciprocal Teaching

Like "Request," reciprocal teaching involves teacher modeling and role reversal; however, this version concentrates more on questioning and summarizing (Palinscar and Brown 1984, 1986). The teacher leads a discussion of why a text may be difficult to understand and what strategic approach to reading may be useful. In addition, the teacher encourages discussion of the role questioning plays in our lives and gradually guides students through the process of asking questions, summarizing information, clarifying, and predicting what the author will say next.

FLUENCY

As their reading fluency increases, learners are able to apply the skills and strategies they have learned in individually determined ways. As students become more fluent readers, teachers should emphasize strategies but they should also provide opportunities for students to explore and experiment with ideas.

Learning Logs

To encourage students to be reflective, Harste, Short, and Burke (1988) suggest a daily learning log, a notebook in which students write about what they are learning. Learning logs can take several different formats: Literature Logs for writing about novels and poems; Observation Logs for documenting observations and scientific experiments; and Learning Logs for science, social studies, and similar content areas.

Literary Discussion

As Lee Gunderson (1995) reminds us, not all reading should be for critical analysis or an exercise to increase comprehension. Learners need time to appreciate good literature as a "whole." Opportunities should be provided for getting together to talk about the books they really enjoyed reading. This means without grades, because as Gunderson (1995) asks, "how do we assess a student's love for a particular book, or for literature in general?" (p. 25).

Literature Circles

Literature circles, as described by Harste, Short, and Burke (1988), help to integrate the reader's ideas with the author's. Literature circles require multiple copies of books; once these have been gathered, the teacher gives a "book talk" about each book so that students can select one based on their personal interests. After they have chosen a book, students read silently. When everyone is finished, those who have read the same book form a literature circle. Open-ended questions can start the discussion: What is this book about? What was your favorite part? Who was your favorite character? A culminating activity can be some type of presentation—a dramatic or musical production, an art display, a book, a poem, or a game—to the whole class.

Teachers sometimes report that older students with reading difficulties benefit little from literature circles because the books that interest them are above their reading level. If this is the case, tape the book and allow the student to read while listening over headphones or ask parents to read the book with their child at home. Chapter 12 describes this process in more detail.

Author's Chair

When students have completed or nearly completed a written piece, they can read it aloud to an audience from the "author's chair" (Harste, Short, and Burke 1988). This is one way to get a constructive response to what they have written. The writer benefits and students have a chance to discuss writing.

Activity Centers

Activity centers help students experiment with putting together and interpreting ideas and accommodate diverse student interests and abilities. Such activities may include

- changing genres: a poem to a story; a story to a play
- retelling or rewriting a story in the style of a TV or newspaper reporter

- creating a game based on the story
- illustrating a story
- creating a script for characters in a story who are being interviewed for a TV show (Gunderson 1995, pp. 42–43).

IN CLOSING

Literacy development is not the accumulation of a sequence of specific skills. Educational philosophy is shifting from the "relief or rescue" approach that ensures classroom homogeneity to the inclusion of all learners, which, in effect, creates diverse classroom communities. To serve groups of learners whose literacy development ranges from emergent to fluent, it is now more important than ever to focus on the learners' needs rather than on curriculum that promotes discrete skills within the artificial construct of "scope and sequence." Learners need immersion in language, demonstrations of strategies and activities, and meaningful opportunities to practice and advance their literacy development.

Self-Directed Learners

As special learners become more comfortable with their own growing literacy, it is not unusual to observe "whole language" teachers moving *toward* a literate environment in which students can stretch their thinking and their feeling. The environment is shaped more by self-motivation and the exchange of ideas among the learners themselves than by the physical properties of the classroom or class routines. Teachers of students who have underdeveloped thinking skills may find the notions of self-motivation and exchanging ideas an idealistic—perhaps even an unreachable—goal.

RESPONSIBILITY AND INDEPENDENCE

As I visit with teachers contemplating the implications of whole language, I often hear their doubts about its workability with their particular students. They are not sure implementing a whole language approach is doable. They tend to believe that students with disabilities lack the skills to be independent learners. They say,

- My students' reading ability is too low to participate in group activities.
- My students won't contribute to a class discussion. They won't even ask questions.
- My students hate to write. It's like pulling teeth to get them to write a sentence.
- My students prefer to work in workbooks. Real reading and writing is too hard, even if it's something in which they are interested.
- My students can't control their behavior well enough to work with somebody or have freedom to walk around the room.

These statements and other, similar observations are probably true more often than not. But they also reveal how some students have traditionally been treated as learners. All learners need to monitor and evaluate their own learning and their own behavior. All learners need to be given choices. How can we expect learners, with or without disabilities, to achieve any degree of responsibility or independence if they are not allowed to develop these traits as they learn? If students do not have these monitoring and evaluation skills, asking them to take responsibility for their own learning and their own behavior will be frightening to them. The teacher's job is to guide them gently toward these goals.

Managing Choices

As we have seen, a basic whole language belief is that learners need to have some choice about what they will learn and how they will learn. For all of us, making a choice can be a difficult task; sometimes we might even wish that someone else would decide for us so we don't have to be responsible for the consequences. In the same way, children may not want to make learning decisions because they have never done it and lack confidence in their ability. Again, teachers need to guide learners through the process. Here are some suggestions.

- If they are to make learning choices through learning center activities, children should first spend a little time at each center. Later they can engage in an activity of their choice.
- Make choices related to consequences: "Dan, I notice you are not working at a center. You may choose to work now or during recess."
- Begin with two or three ideas for a unit of study and let students vote on their preference.
- Provide students with a variety of books to choose during free reading time. Give book talks to pique student interest.
- At the beginning of the class, post and discuss the day's learning activities and tasks that students are responsible for accomplishing. Include one or two options and allow students to decide the order in which to complete them.

Risk Taking

Another important aspect of the whole language philosophy is risk taking, which is possible only in an atmosphere of trust. Learners will take risks if they trust that their teacher will not humiliate them, punish them, or penalize them for making mistakes.

In *Strategies That Inspire Students,* Merrill Harmin (1993) discusses what he calls "truths" that encourage an atmosphere of trust. He suggests that teachers post "truth signs" such as:

- Everyone needs time to think and learn.
- We learn in our own way and according to our own timeclock.
- It's okay to make mistakes. That's the way we learn.
- We can accept and support one another. No one needs to feel alone.
- We can do more and learn more when we are willing to take risks.

The teacher should not simply post these signs, she should discuss their implications. And in discussing risk taking with students, it is important to distinguish between "smart risks" and "dangerous risks." In order to keep these truths a vital part of the classroom philosophy, Harmin advises giving a "steady offering of reminders and support" (p. 51), asking, for example, "Is it okay if someone gives a wrong answer? Why? Is it okay if you don't understand everything?" This helps students relax and develop self-confidence.

SELF-DIRECTED FORMATS

Teachers of learners with disabilities who trust in their students' ability to learn have successfully adopted and adapted formats used in general education whole language classrooms to develop self-directed learners. Two particularly effective structures are literature circles and workshops.

Literature Circles

Literature circles allow learners to experience reading as pleasurable by giving them opportunities to savor and share their reading (Keefe, in press). In its basic form, a literature circle comprises students who are in the process of reading the same trade book, the same article, or books on the same theme. They read and talk about what they have read. An important feature is the participation and responses of group members as they discuss, evaluate, and analyze characters and situations in the text and then take these experiences beyond the text into their own lives. Literature circles, then, are a classroom version of what readers like to do—talk about what they read with others. Adults do this informally with friends or formally as members of book clubs or literary discussion groups.

Although the literature circle idea has been integrated into many class-rooms since the 1980s, many teachers may not be comfortable with the format, perhaps because it entails a change in roles for both the teacher and students. If literature circles are to be successful, teachers must let go of their authoritarian role as "teller of what you should know." As Harvey Daniels (1994) points out, the teacher becomes an organizer, a manager, a locator of materials, an observer, and an evaluator. But the teacher also becomes a fellow reader and "a powerful demonstrator of how mature readers really think" (p. 26).

As the teacher lets go of control, the students take charge of their reading and discussion. To guide students toward meaningful and productive discussions, teachers often ask students to perform a job or a role in their group. These might include

Facilitator: Makes sure everyone has an opportunity to participate.
Discussion Director: Convenes group meetings and asks open-ended questions, such as, "What did you think about . . .?"
Secretary: Records important ideas or pages for reading assignment
Reader: Picks out passages to read aloud.
Word Detective: Picks out words from the reading to discuss.
AV Person: Sets up tape recorder if meeting is to be recorded.
Wrap-up Person: Summarizes what happens or makes sure the discussion ends in an orderly fashion.

In this way, students are able to take ownership of their groups; they make their own reading assignments and discuss what they perceive as relevant. Within the literature circle, expectations change. Students no longer answer a predetermined set of questions; rather, as individuals they are expected to be contributing members of their group, and as a collective group they are expected to broaden their understanding of what they are reading.

Of course, we cannot expect that simply setting up literature circles will stimulate insightful discussion. Students who have received a remedial reading instruction have been inundated with sight vocabulary and decoding skill exercises, but the closest they have come to real reading may be a basal reader with, of course, the obligatory comprehension questions. In other words, students in remedial programs usually have little or no opportunity to engage in authentic reading. Perhaps they have never seen anyone read for pleasure, and because reading discussion has always occurred in the context of answering comprehension questions, they may never have observed meaningful discussion. Careful preparation is necessary. Here are steps to encourage students to become engaged in literature circles:

Step 1. Demonstrate discussions of literature.

- When reading aloud to students, integrate new information with old information ("This reminds me of the story we read last week"); make predictions about the story and ask students to make predictions.
- Describe the use of visual imagery. Ask students to close their eyes while a passage is read out loud. Invite them to "see" what is being described in their minds. Afterwards, ask them about color, scenery, clothing, and other details that were not mentioned in the written text. Compare their answers and discuss how different readers create different images in their "mind's eye."
- Demonstrate a discussion of a book or a TV program familiar to the students with another adult. Ask students to brainstorm to make a list of the kinds of things that were discussed:

    the characters
    likable characters and why they were likable
    unlikable characters and why they were unlikable
    favorite parts of the book
    least favorite parts of the book
    funny/scary/sad scenes
    parts that should be changed

Step 2. Introduce literature circles. Explain to students not only what they will be doing but also why they will be doing it. I usually describe how I feel when I can share my thoughts about a book with a friend who is also reading it.

Step 3. Introduce the roles students will perform. After introducing the job roles (facilitator, reading, AV person, and so on), give students a short story to read. Next demonstrate the various jobs and create role-playing situations so students can practice. Later students will choose jobs they will perform within the group.

Step 4. Help students develop cooperative group skills. Group assignments have become a popular teaching strategy because they introduce cooperative planning and group problem solving. These skills are highly valued in our society—much of what we do as adults, we do cooperatively with other adults. Group projects may not be beneficial, however, if learners are not adequately prepared to work in a group. Social skills are the most important ingredient in successful group work. If group members don't know how to listen to others and share their ideas effectively, the group will not function well. It is important to discuss your expectations for group behavior and group processes beforehand. Make sure, for example, that students perceive a literature group as a mini-community: members should make space for everyone in the group, call each other by name, stay with the group, and make eye contact when they speak to another group member. Demonstrating how to listen and how to take turns will be time well spent, and it should continue until students clearly understand what is expected. Do not give up group work because students seem to lack the appropriate skills. They can only develop these skills if they can practice them. If there are instances when conflicting personalities disrupt the group so that it cannot function, it is wise to separate these individuals from each other (see Chapter 14 for further discussion of this topic).

Step 5. Introduce books with a "book talk." Briefly describe the plot of each book, which may share a common title, author, or theme. Allow students to browse through the books and then ask them to write down their first and second choices. Explain that the number of students in a group cannot exceed the number of copies of the book.

Step 6. Form groups. Form small groups (3–4) according to book selection to encourage more individual participation. During the first meeting, ask students to discuss why they chose the title they did and what they think it will be about. They also need to decide how much of the book they should read for the next meeting. Ask students to decide which jobs they will perform. A group job sheet listing rotating job assignments will help students focus on what they need to accomplish (Keegan and Shrake 1991).

Less Able Readers

The literature circle is a natural support system, but teachers who have students with multilevel abilities and general education teachers who have inclusive classrooms may be hesitant about including students with disabilities in these groups. They may be concerned that

- Students may not be able to read well enough to keep up with the group or may choose a book they cannot actually read.
- Students will not engage in discussion.
- Students do not know how to work in a group.
- They cannot adequately supervise the groups.

These are legitimate reservations. Such problems can create obstacles that make literature circles uninviting. Involving students with drastically different reading abilities may seem to undermine the idea of meaningful interaction among the students. Including students who have reading abilities substantially lower than other group members is a challenge, but it is not impossible. Keep in mind the inherent support group members offer each other. Not only should teachers recognize this support system, but the students should understand that, as members of a community of readers, one of their responsibilities is to give and receive help.

Students who cannot read the selected book independently may need additional support. Here are several alternatives:

- The teacher, a paraprofessional, or a volunteer can read a portion of the book aloud as students follow along.
- Students can read along with a buddy.
- A parent, volunteer, or older student can tape the book, if it is not already available on audiotape, so students can listen over headphones and follow along.
- Parents can read the book to their child at home.
- If the group is reading thematic books, they should reflect a variety of reading levels. (If less able readers select a book that is not on their reading level, encourage them to do so.)

Suggesting alternative reading methods to less able readers may be a delicate situation. Present a variety of solutions and let the student decide the most appropriate method. Reading along with a classmate (buddy reading) may be very stigmatizing for one student, while another may prefer it to listening to a tape with headphones or having parents read aloud at home.

The control issue is another obstacle. Sometimes special education teachers feel an even greater need to be in control of their students than general education teachers. To help alleviate anxiety about students' ability to stay on task, teachers might try giving them a time frame in which to accomplish certain activities: for example, "By Wednesday all group members should be finished reading Chapter 1 and be ready to discuss." Gradually, as they become more self-directed and the teacher learns to trust them, students will make these decisions themselves.

Because the teacher cannot physically observe every group all the time, it may be beneficial to ask each group to tape-record discussions. Students may also need some assistance in organizing and structuring group meetings.

Managing Discussion Groups

In the beginning, teachers should make an effort to sit in on each group as a careful listener. The teacher should listen for kernels of ideas and help students expand them, make statements rather than ask questions, and, most important, be nonjudgmental. Of course, not all discussions will last the same amount of time. It is a good idea to have a list of activities students can pursue while other groups are finishing: write in response journal, do research, read a book, browse, work at the computer, and so on. When students have finished reading their books, a culminating project is a nice finale. It can be an art project, a dramatization, a poster depicting major events, an original poem or song, a board game, or a panel discussion. A project allows students to tap their creativity, extend their understanding, and share what they have experienced with students outside their group. A project also keeps students engaged while other groups are finishing their books.

Evaluation

Because teachers relinquish their position as the primary informer, they have more time to use qualitative evaluation methods (see Chapter 7). But it is also important for students to evaluate themselves. Many teachers find that a response journal is a good way for students to reflect on their feelings as they read. With young students, or students who are not very adept at this type of writing, a typical response may be something like, "I read pp. 2–6. It was good." I would suggest that teachers demonstrate writing a response entry every day about something they are actually reading. It can be done on the chalkboard or on chart paper so everyone can watch and listen. The teacher might think aloud:

I wonder what ———— means?
I like the character of ————. She reminds me of ———— because ————.

My favorite part so far is ————.

One Teacher's Literature Study Groups

Teresa Degrand decided that she needed to change the reading program for her fifth- and sixth-grade students with learning disabilities. "I needed to change or quit teaching—the students weren't progressing," she said. She was using a basal series with typical workbook exercises and decided to switch to a literature-based program using novels. Her students all read the same novel and discussed it in a "teacher asks questions—student answers" format. But this, she felt, was too teacher-directed; she wanted her students to be more engaged in the literature. She began experimenting with literature circles. In the beginning, she grouped students according to their reading ability and chose theme-study-related books for them to read. They read, responded in their journals, and shared their responses with the other class members. Teresa still wasn't satisfied. She wanted them to have an interactive discussion with each other.

Using suggestions from Keegan and Shrake (1991), Teresa made the literature groups more learner directed. First, she created group reading folders, each of which contained a job sheet, an assignment sheet, discussion questions, and teacher feedback. Now the literature groups pick up their folder each day and check the job sheet.

Job Sheet

R (Reader): Reads teacher's comments to the group and discussion
    questions aloud.
M (Mechanic): Sets up the tape recorder.
C (Coordinator): Makes sure everyone has a chance to talk. Keeps the
    group on track.
S (Secretary): Writes down reading assignment.

Date	R	M	C	S
11/21	Brad	Joel	Sue	Cassie
11/22	Sue	Cassie	Brad	Joel

Next, the group members decide how many pages or chapters of their books they will read. The assignment can be the same for the entire group or different for an individual who reads at a slower rate. Members also have to take into consideration the time they need to discuss their reading and respond in their journals. In addition, they jointly decide whether they will read silently, read aloud in a group, or read with a buddy. (The students I interviewed reported that they based their decision mostly on "what kind of mood they're in.")

Assignment Sheet
Book Title:

Date	Group members	Assignment
11/21	Brad	pp. 20–27
	Sue	"
	Cassie	"
	Joel	"

Next, the "Reader" reads the teacher's comments on the previous group session.

Teacher's Comments

11/19 Your discussions went well. I like the way all of you participated. Keep up the good work.

11/20 Excellent job of deciding how much to read. This is a successful group.

11/21 I like the way you thought of your own questions to ask. Be sure to always take turns.

11/22 I liked being in your group today. I liked the way you compared the book to a TV program you watched.

When every student in the group has completed the reading assignment they go to their designated area to discuss it. Students who finish reading early usually go to the reading corner and browse until everyone has finished.

Teresa's goal is to allow the groups to discuss their reading with little or no teacher direction. In the beginning, however, she furnished them with prompt questions to stimulate their discussion.

Discussion Questions

11/19

Where and when does the story take place? How do you know? If the story took place somewhere else or in a different time, how would the story change?

Who is the main character? What kind of person is he/she? How do you know?

How would you change the character?

Did the chapter end the way you thought?

What was your favorite part?

Would you leave any part out?

Would you add anything?

Teresa is a guest member in one group every day. When she does not sit in on a group, the group tape-records their discussion. At a later time (usually during recess) she listens to the tape and comments.

When students finish their discussion, they respond individually in their journals. Teresa has spent time with them discussing the different kinds of responses they can make. A chart displayed on the wall lists ideas. Here is an example of a student response:

> I thot the Indians were going to stel ther fer. But they got cot by there chef and they had to put the fer back.

Finally, if there is time, the students go to an area that resembles a cozy living room. A large chair, the "Author's Chair," sits apart from the others. Students take turn sitting in the Author's Chair and sharing what they have written in their journals.

As I observed the students, they seemed very confident about the procedure and indicated that they enjoyed the literature groups. As Teresa has discovered, her students now love to read, whereas in the past they did not. She says, "They get so excited when we get a book order. They act like it's Christmas!"

By participating in literature discussion groups children listen to other readers' ideas, share their favorite parts with an interested audience, and express emotions they felt as they read. Most important, they share the pleasures of reading. This may be the only opportunity children from literacy-deprived homes have to share the joy of reading.

Workshops

Reading and Writing Workshop

The workshop format, popularized by Donald Graves (1983), Nancie Atwell (1987), and Jane Hansen (1987), is intended to foster productive reading and writing. The "workshop" metaphor conveys the message that a community of learners is working toward set goals and outcomes. Many teachers find the workshop format an ideal way to organize learners' activities while still giving them choice and responsibility.

In a workshop environment, the physical arrangement of classroom furniture and materials intentionally promotes interaction. The teacher can meet with individual students in small conference areas, and a larger area encourages whole class meetings to share particular accomplishments or works in progress. The teacher is thus a facilitator, not a director.

Workshop Structure. Teacher and students together establish rules to fit their own particular circumstances and needs (one rule, for example, might be that the workshop is not a time to do homework). Next, they set up a schedule. The following time frame is modeled after Nancie Atwell's description of her workshops in *In the Middle:*

Status of work (5 minutes): Students briefly state what they plan to read or what writing piece they will work on.

Mini-lesson (5–10 minutes): Mini-lessons are scheduled as needed. The teacher might generate a discussion about a literary topic (such as the ingredients of a humorous story) one day or a specific technical topic (such as the use of quotation marks) on another.

Reading/Writing time (35–45 minutes): While students read or write, the teacher moves around the class giving help, answering questions, or settling students down. The teacher may act as an advisor by suggesting alternatives, or serve as a guide to resources. If the teacher takes time to read or write, students will see that she values language as a fellow member of the classroom reading and writing community.

Sharing (5–10 minutes): Sharing time is also scheduled as necessary. Some teachers like to use a sign-up sheet. Sharing is voluntary, not required.

Dialogue Journal. A dialogue journal serves as a tangible example of students' reflections, reactions, and responses. Students exchange their journals with the teacher or other students, who respond in writing. The teacher can use the dialogue format to question, prod, or challenge as appropriate. Some teachers like to have students write on loose-leaf paper, which they keep in a three-ring binder, so they do not have to part with their whole journal at one time and may submit selected responses according to a set schedule. Other teachers prefer spiral notebooks, which lessen the chance that responses will be misplaced, so that they can review student responses over time. The teacher may need to build in time to read the students' journals and respond to their writing before the next workshop.

These organizing structures of the workshop may be dropped as soon as students become comfortable with routine. More mature readers and writers may simply read and write for the whole period.

Teachers who work with children with special needs find the workshop format appealing because it allows one-on-one interaction between student and teacher. Melissa Taylor, who teaches students with behavioral disorders, incorporated both a reading workshop and literature sets into her reading program. She organized the workshop as follows:

1. Read a book of your choice for thirty minutes each day.
2. Respond to the book in your reading response log every day.
3. Keep a running list of the books you have read.
4. Complete a final project at the end of each book.

Final projects were student selected and could be an original idea or one from a number that Melissa provided. These projects included oral reports, reports written on the computer, another version of the book read, student-designed T-shirts illustrating the book, letters to the authors, and dioramas.

Melissa first experimented with reading workshops in a class of ten intermediate-aged students (nine boys, one girl) with behavioral disorders. She discovered that implementing a whole language philosophy did not interfere with the behavior management system that she used in her classroom. She still expected students to behave appropriately at all times. She continued to use the established behavior management system and felt that this consistency allowed students to succeed in less-structured activities. She also felt that the workshop activities prepared students to extend their academic time in general education classrooms.

As Melissa's students read more and more books, their excitement was palpable. Throughout the year they all expressed a growing love of reading. On its own, this would have been enough to convince Melissa that a steady diet of good literature was beneficial; at the same time, however, their comprehension became better, their reading fluency improved, and their vocabulary increased. And because she combined reading and writing, her students became active writers as well.

As a resource teacher for grades 6–12, Rachael Hobbs scheduled both a reading and a writing workshop: two days of reading, two days of writing, and one day of working on a special project. Because the students came to Rachael's classroom for only an hour a day, they had to use their time efficiently. When Rachael first introduced the workshop format, she fused it with a year-long theme study of medieval times. One interesting component of her workshop was the read-aloud period. At the beginning of the class, the students went to the reading area—three sofas arranged to enhance conversation and a book-shelf full of books. Rachael read aloud to her students to demonstrate good reading and while reading she also incorporated mini-lessons about writing. On a day when I was observing in her classroom, she was reading a story about the Pied Piper of Hamlin and came to a passage that vividly described one of the characters. After she read it, she stopped to talk about the author's use of adjectives to give readers a mental picture of the character. Then she reread the passage, eliminating all the adjectives, and the students discussed how lifeless it was without them. In a rather offhand manner, Rachael suggested that they might want to think about using adjectives in their own writing and continued the reading.

Like Melissa, Rachael found that her emphasis on reading literature and writing paid off. Although she did not do much "tutoring," and the resource room was not a place to do homework, students' immersion and engagement in a literate environment became evident in their content area classes. They were better able to read the content area textbooks, more confident about taking part in class discussions, and they began to see school as a worthwhile endeavor—the majority of her resource students were beginning to make plans to attend college!

Arts Workshop

Learners who have difficulty with the alphabetic code may enjoy literacy more fully through art mediums. They may willingly draw, act or sing when given the opportunity—or they may not if it is a new experience. Many teachers include the arts in their curriculum either regularly or occasionally. Unfortunately, in some quarters, the arts are considered "nonacademic" and unnecessary to the education of a "worthy" citizen. I would suggest, however, that an art project is a legitimate "academic" endeavor: it requires perceiving relationships, drawing on prior knowledge, solving problems, and monitoring progress.

"School art" usually refers to drawing or painting a picture. Yet, knowing that all art forms can be vehicles for expressing literacy and thinking skills and that teachers feel pressed for time, I developed the idea of an arts workshop based on the reading and writing workshop model. I asked a few teachers to try it out, and they began doing an arts workshop once a week, usually on Friday. Sometimes the activities were related to a theme, or a book students were reading, but just as often they were not. The basic goals of the arts workshop were to demonstrate that art surrounds us every where and to encourage students to experiment with various art forms.

In the first weeks of the workshop, we introduced students to the arts as a whole: visual arts, drama, music, and dance/movement. We decided it might be a good idea to invite guest artists to talk and demonstrate their art. However, as we explored the local library and other resources, we discovered many activities we could share with the students that didn't require "expertise."

The next segment was designed to explore a variety of art forms in more depth. As an introduction to each art form, we provided some type of demonstration. When possible field trips were taken or resident artists were invited to share their craft. For example, I was invited to demonstrate the art of pantomime using the familiar story of "Goldilocks and the Three Bears," but I did not tell students the name of the story in advance. As part of my introduction I discussed "illusion"—seeing things with our mind's eye. After I had pantomimed the story, the children excitedly called out names. Someone said, "Little Red Riding Hood." Then, "No, it's about the Three Bears." "Oh yeah, the little girl with blond hair." "Goldilocks!"

I asked the children if they could tell me what they "saw" happen in their mind's eye. As they retold the story, I asked them to explain how they knew what was happening. For example, when one little girl said, "Goldilocks tasted the soup and it was too hot," I asked, "How did you know it was too hot?" She explained how my facial expressions and gestures had communicated "hot." Through this kind of probing I realized that these children (some of whom had been identified as communication disordered) were well able to comprehend a story through body language, facial expressions, and their imaginations, putting into practice a literacy skill they had no doubt developed long before coming to school.

Then the children had an opportunity to create their own mime illusions. First, each student handled a real ball, a real fork, and a real glass. I asked them, as they felt the objects, to think about space, weight, and texture: How big is it? How heavy is it? How does it feel to the touch? Next, we stood in a circle and passed around imaginary objects, such as a basketball, a snake, an egg, a giant bubble, and a heavy box. The students also engaged in other mime activities, such as climbing a fence, diving, and digging a hole. No one refused to participate. In fact, they came up with their own illusions (they loved using this word). Barb Kinsella's class loved it so much that they asked to pantomime their favorites among the stories Barb read aloud to them. Without any teacher direction they formed three groups, chose a story, went to separate corners of the room to rehearse, and soon were ready to perform. I was quite amazed at the ease with which they organized these performances, and Barb was surprised at how well they depicted the plots and the characters. My guess is that some of them were quite experienced because playacting had probably been a big part of their play but was something they did not often get to exhibit at school.

After these introductory demonstrations came "Art Talk," a time when we introduced several activities based on the target art form. These activities can become the organizing principle for various centers around the room, and students can choose to participate in one or several. Examples of centers are:

Painting/Drawing: several areas in the room with painter's smocks, brushes, paper. Each area has a different medium: oil paint, acrylic, fingerpaint, watercolor, charcoal, pastels.

Music: several centers spotlight different musical instruments: keyboards, tambourine, ukelele, guitar, drums. Other centers have headphones with various recordings: classical music, marches, music of different countries and cultures.

Crafts: several centers with materials to make holiday decorations.
Drama: several centers for playwriting, costume design, set design.

Some extension activities for the pantomime demonstration included the following:

- Mime a familiar story for the class.
- Choose an object in the classroom to observe. Notice its color, size, length, weight, and feel. Describe the object orally or in writing.
- Mime a situation for a group (such as being trapped in a box, running from someone, burning your hand on a hot pan). Use the following questions to develop a group story:

  What happened before the incident?
  How did the individual feel during the incident?
  How did the individual feel after the incident?
  What might happen next?

- Research the history of pantomime.
- Create a pantomime alphabet book. Let students photograph each other pantomiming a word for each letter of the alphabet (A/antelope, B/bounce, C/cat, and so on).

Students need not stay within the boundaries of the activities in the centers. Often they develop their own projects. The format of the arts workshop can be the same as that of the reading/writing workshop:

Art talk: The teacher shares a "how-to," a brief biographical sketch of an artist, an explanation of a style, a genre, a technique.
Work time: Students work on their projects. The teacher, also engaged in a project, moves around, assists, and answers questions.
Artist on stage: Students share their finished artwork or performance.

A workshop structure for introducing and exploring the arts offers tremendous benefits. First, it exposes learners to a variety of art forms and provides an opportunity for self-expression and self-acceptance. Learners become aware of the endless avenues for communicating ideas and discover another entry point into learning they might not otherwise have encountered.

Literature circles and workshops offer workable structures for a learner-centered environment that fosters self-directed rather than teacher-directed learning. Supportive contexts such as these assist learners who have become passive or dependent on their teachers to spoon feed information to them.

Learner-Centered Curriculum

Allowing students to take responsibility for their own learning may be a difficult transition for many teachers to make. Even more difficult is allowing students to choose the content of the curriculum. When the teacher becomes facilitator of the curriculum rather than its author, learning activities are less contrived and less controlled, and there is more authentic reading and more genuine inquiry. At the same time, a learning community develops in which students have a voice in how they will learn (this is the really scary part) and share in the responsibility and the work.

Now for a reality check. This all sounds wonderful, of course, but the truth of the matter is that kids who have spent a great deal of time in special education, or who have been spoon-fed for years, may not be ready for such active learning. After all, a great deal of research tells us that a high percentage of learners in special education are passive and are not the greatest problem solvers. How do we confront the problems inherent in the learning characteristics of students with disabilities? First, let us revisit Brian Cambourne's (1988) conditions for learning: immersion, demonstration, expectation, responsibility, use, approximation, and response—all accompanied by engagement. A key condition at this point is *demonstration accompanied by engagement*. Learners must see many demonstrations they can regard as *doable*. I also believe that demonstrations are much more likely to be viewed as doable if the teacher actually demonstrates rather than models. A demonstration includes making mistakes, noticing mistakes, correcting mistakes, and other kinds of problem solving. Modeling, in contrast, is carrying out an activity with no apparent struggle or problem solving.

If learners are used to being passive, the teacher may have to do a lot of suggesting and coercing at the start, while they contribute what and when they can. After a while, they will become more independent. Here are some examples of how several teachers approached learner-centered curriculums.

Cathy Neidhardt: Teacher of students, ages 9–12, with moderate to severe behavioral problems and reading abilities ranging from first to beginning of fourth grade.

Because choosing a topic to study was a new experience for her class, Cathy got the ball rolling by selecting a general one—the rain forest—and reading *The Great Kapok Tree* by Cherry Lynne (1990). She told the class that if this topic didn't interest them, they could investigate another one. The students enjoyed listening to Cathy read the book and pointed out aspects of the illustrations she had not noticed, such as animals hiding in the forest. After reading the book, she asked the students what they might like to learn about. The class brainstormed and decided they wanted to know more about the following animals: toucan, sloth, arrow poison frog, jaguar, pufferbird, tamarin, and bluebird. They each (including Cathy) chose one animal to study and brainstormed questions they wanted answered:

What do they look like?
How long do they live?
What do they do?
What food do they eat?
Do they have fun? How?
What is their protection?
Who/what are their enemies?

To give them more background information, Cathy read them other books about the rain forest. Then she asked students to write down everything they knew so far about their chosen animal. This would give them a starting point for determining what they still needed to find out. Cathy explained to them that they would be writing an informational report about their animal later in the month, which they would share with other class members, and, if they wanted, with other classes.

The students discussed how to get information about their topics. They gathered in pairs or threes to list the people and resources that might provide information. They all needed help getting started. Cathy was not surprised because they were undertaking a new process and previously she had always been their primary informant. Once they received a little help, they had no difficulty in coming up with ideas. They were, however, very concerned about their spelling, and Cathy took the opportunity to discuss different kinds of writing and the purposes of each kind. She explained that the list was for their own personal use; if they knew what it said, spelling wasn't a significant issue. It was an important clarification because worry about spelling seemed to dam the flow of ideas.

Not only were the students responsible for assembling a list of potential resources, they also were responsible for actually locating the people and places and making phone calls. These tasks led quite naturally to a lesson about how to find names and places in the phone book. Another natural outcome was learning to share the phone book. The solution was to take turns: one group member found the number while another wrote it down.

In order to help students make successful phone calls, Cathy gave a demonstration, and she wrote on the chalkboard what she would ordinarily write down on a piece of paper before picking up the phone. The students also role-played making phone calls. Most of them used Cathy's basic format. "My name is ——— from ——— School. We are studying rain forests and I was wondering if you had any information about ———." When the students actually made their phone calls, Cathy was surprised at how well they did. They were able to say their introductions, listen to responses, answer questions, and politely sign off. Only one student handed the phone to Cathy—he got a recorded message and didn't know what to do! Most students asked to get information sent; however, one student, who called the local library to ask for information, ended up making an appointment for the whole class to visit during a time when the librarian could help them.

The library visit turned out to be a wonderful experience for Cathy and her students because they learned how to use the computer to locate their books. The students were quite excited about finding their books, and their excitement continued when they brought the books back to the classroom and began exploring them for information.

The "Animals in the Rain Forest" study involved a variety of activities. Some were generated by Cathy, but the students also generated their own. A debate occurred, for example, over whether or not the boa constrictor would eat a tamarin monkey. The student "expert" on boas believed the boa would eat the tamarin, since its prey includes small mammals. However, the expert on tamarins felt that because the tamarin is a good climber and fast, the boa would not be able to catch it. Both backed up their opinions with facts.

Throughout their study, the students talked about the size of their animals. They wanted to see just how big or how little the animals were. Cathy left it up to them to decide how they would accomplish this goal. The boa expert decided to roll up paper and put it end to end: he discovered that a sheet of paper was one foot long, so he needed eighteen pieces. Two other students decided to draw a line on the chalkboard showing the length of the toucan. They also added the length of its beak, which is as big as its body! Another cut out a piece of paper to show the size of the bluebird.

At the end of the unit, the students wanted to see their animals in real life. While Cathy couldn't arrange a trip to a rain forest, she did take them to the zoo, where they viewed the poison arrow frog, the boa constrictor, the toucan, the bluebird, and the tamarin. Although the students had seen numerous pictures of their animals and had tried to represent their size, they were surprised to see their actual size and color.

Overall, Cathy was very pleased with the rain forest unit. The students became very active in their learning: they looked at books during their free time, talked with each other about the rain forest, discussed their work with support staff, and brought information from home. In addition, they were reading and writing for their own purposes. Their learning was more purposeful, Cathy felt, because they had an active voice in what they learned and how they learned it.

Margaret Snyder: Teacher of high school students with behavioral disorders.

Margaret admits that she was skeptical about doing a learner-directed unit of study but decided to try it out in her English class. She introduced the idea as "something cool I'm learning about in my college class." Having gotten their attention, she explained to the students that they could actually choose what they wanted to study based on a general theme. As a group they decided to study the ocean, and they spent a class period brainstorming and mapping ideas on the board. At first they were hesitant about contributing, but then a spark seemed to light and they filled the board with ideas: sea life, sea shells, oil spills, the Bermuda Triangle, scuba diving, sunken treasures, coral reefs, the

Titanic, ghosts and myths, hurricanes, and many others. Each student chose something in which they had a particular interest to study.

Margaret then led them in a discussion about how to investigate their topics and present their findings. This was a little more difficult because they didn't have much experience in researching, but Margaret made a few suggestions, and they were able to come up with more ideas on their own: inviting guest speakers, reading books, looking at pictures and photographs, and interviewing experts. Their methods of presentation would include posters, written reports, drawings, diagrams, oral reports, games, skits, art, music, videos, collage, newspaper articles, and cooking. Margaret brought in books from the library, and as students perused them, she held individual conferences to discuss topics of interest and ideas for a class project.

The students chose the following activities:

Mandy: Wrote a report about coral reefs and created a bulletin board with both hand-drawn and magazine pictures of fish, shells, mollusks, and plants. As a final touch she covered the bulletin board with blue plastic wrap. She received a lot of help from class members and nonclass members, who thought is was a "neat" idea.

Nathan and Mark: As a team they decided to investigate specific occurrences in the area of the Bermuda Triangle. They completed a time line, a freehand map, a drawing of a ghost ship with a story about it, and a poster with a write-up about sea monsters entitled, "The Past," which described what people used to think happened to missing ships. They also presented a lesson to the class: They read aloud a story about the Bermuda Triangle, led a group discussion, reviewed some vocabulary words, and had students complete comprehension questions. Next, they brought in a videotaped program about the Bermuda Triangle. Finally, they asked students to list ten facts they had learned about the Bermuda Triangle.

Adam: Intended to invite a scuba diver to speak to the class and make a poster showing scuba diving gear. However, he was not able to contact the intended guest speaker or find the "really great book" that described all the gear. He did spend several days reading about scuba diving for treasure and copying information from the book. Margaret nudged him a little by having him make a list of facts. Using the list, he was able to write a one-page report about places to go in the Caribbean to dive for treasure and also labeled and colored a map of the area and drew in the routes of merchant ships of long ago.

Paul and Jesse: Intended to write a report about the *Titanic,* create maps and pictures, and give an oral presentation to the class. However, the two got into an argument on the second day, refused to work with one another, and ended up doing separate projects. Jesse skimmed a few books about the *Titanic* and partially completed a map of the area and a picture of the tiny submarine that was used to investigate the wreckage. Paul helped Mandy some with the bulletin board and then began to work on the topic of speedboats, but he was not really able to complete anything due to absences.

Gary: Intended to bring in books about deep-sea fishing, but he stopped coming to school.

Andy: Was interested in myths and ghost stories in additional books, but he dropped out of school.

When the students had completed these projects, Margaret gave them the choice of continuing to explore the ocean or going back to the materials they were using earlier. Most of them wanted to keep working on the ocean topic; however, a few, who had been absent during most of the theme study, wanted to work with the standard materials. During this second round, Mandy completed a Venn diagram comparing and contrasting dolphins and porpoises along with a collage and a written report, which she presented to the class. Nathan also did a Venn diagram comparing hydrofoils and Hovercrafts. Adam completed a picture of an aircraft carrier and a written report which he presented orally to the class. Paul wrote a report on nuclear submarines accompanied by pictures of the different types of missiles found on submarines. A new student, John, read four short stories about the ocean and wrote short summaries stating the main facts on index cards.

One day Margaret brought in dried seaweed. She passed it around and had the students close their eyes and then describe any familiar tastes and smells. Most of them did not like the taste, but they agreed they would eat the seaweed if stranded on an island. The taste experiment triggered their imaginations about being stranded. They formed groups of three to discuss and list the characteristics of their island, such as weather, topography, special land forms, and natural resources. Then they drew maps of their island. As an extension activity, some of the students took the seaweed around to other classes for a taste test, while the others came up with a quick survey about liking or disliking seaweed. The students conducted their survey during lunch break and posted the results on the school's main bulletin board: 97 percent of the people who tried seaweed didn't like it.

The island projects continued as students designed three-dimensional models and brought in needed supplies. Students worked in groups on the various models. They wrapped sheets of wood in aluminum foil, crinkled the foil to make it look like waves, and then covered it in blue plastic wrap. Next, they used newspaper to create papier-mâché islands. Margaret was quite impressed with their organized group effort. Two students ripped up newspaper, while another made the papier-mâché mixture. Three students and a teacher's assistant wrapped the boards with the foil and plastic wrap. Their self-selected project resulted in a natural use of cooperative skills because they all viewed themselves as stakeholders.

After the students finished their island models, they spent time talking about how to live on these islands. They were quite knowledgeable about living off the land. Each group made lists of the natural resources on their island and decided to add the lists to their maps with appropriate symbols. To make it easier to transport goods they decided to build seaports. This project then led them to read Jean Craighead George's *My Side of the Mountain* (1991), a book about a boy who learned to survive in the wilderness.

All in all, Margaret was satisfied with her first experience with a learner-directed unit of study. She was amazed at how one activity flowed into another. The students who were involved were really involved, and those who weren't seemed to notice that they had missed out.

Margaret did have some lingering concerns. One student didn't seem to do well with the lack of structure. He would start projects and then become bored with them and not want to continue. He worked slowly and acted indecisively, although Margaret tried to guide him by suggesting ideas. This isn't an uncommon situation. Not all students will do well with decisions and self-direction the first time they try. But these students do need experience in making choices and directing their own activities. Too many students leave high school overly dependent on extant structures. Students like these need limited choices: for example, "Here are three things you can do; choose one." "Complete [a project] by a certain date." These students need to move gradually toward independence.

Margaret also mentioned that she felt disorganized and not quite "on top of things," but had the feeling that this was all part of the process of letting go of control, of learning to trust the learners.

Christine Wallace Fresen: Middle school instructional/resource teacher.

Christine's first experience with a learner-centered curriculum began somewhat differently: it was more an accident than a well thought-out decision. She was familiar with thematic studies and, in the back of her mind, knew they were something she wanted to experiment with. This is what happened.

One day, Josh, a sixth-grade student, commented that the classroom was so hot it was tropical. Christine asked him if he knew of any tropical places, and he named off Hawaii, Florida, and the Bahamas. All the students in the room joined the conversation, and Christine asked if they would like to learn more about tropical places. Perhaps, she suggested, since the classroom *felt* tropical, they would like to make the classroom *look* tropical as well. The students were very enthusiastic about what they might do. They decided to learn about the Bahamas, because they had seen it advertised as a popular vacation spot.

The students first went to the library to look up the Bahamas, the West Indies, and the Caribbean in the encyclopedias. Through their preliminary reading, each student developed a different interest and chose a different topic to research independently in the encyclopedias, as well as textbooks and library books. They decided to share their knowledge with the whole class by writing a summary. Before Josh wrote his summary of plant life in the Bahamas, he developed a semantic map. Christine had introduced semantic maps earlier in the year and was delighted that he was able to generalize this strategy.

Next, the students decided they could probably find out more by getting brochures from a travel agency. They looked in the phone book to find out which ones were nearby and decided they would call rather than write because it was faster. After rehearsing what to say, Josh volunteered to make the call from the school office. A woman at the travel agency was very helpful, and said she would find out what was available and give Josh a call back. Josh gave her the school phone number. After he hung up the phone, he went to the office and told the school secretary that he was expecting a phone call from the travel agency regarding some travel brochures for his class. The secretary said she would be very happy to take the message for him.

A few days later Christine picked up the brochures from the travel agency and also rented a travel video from a local video store. The brochures and video were very informative. Not only were they useful in writing the summaries, but they also gave students some great ideas for classroom scenery: palm trees, flamingos, a grass hut, and parachuting on the beach.

When the students had finished writing their summaries on the computer, they made several copies and exchanged them with each other. Then they used all the summaries to create their own informational brochure about the Bahamas, complete with illustrations and a cover.

The students in Christine's class became so intrigued with the Bahamas that they decided to produce a videotaped commercial advertising its wonderful attributes. The theme song of the commercial was "Kokomo" by the Beach Boys. They sang the song while demonstrating some of the things one can experience in the Bahamas. They wanted to come out through the door of their grass hut at the beginning of the commercial, but it took too long, so after some discussion, they decided to jump out from behind the hut. Props for the commercial included steel drums made from aluminum foil, a toy saxophone (for the saxophone solo in the song), and an assortment of beach paraphernalia.

The culminating activity for the theme study was a cultural experience party. Students watched their commercial and ate Bahamanian-type food. The students brought in pineapples, kiwis, bananas, mangoes, melons, and coconuts. Christine contributed imitation lobster, shrimp, and crab pieces. The speech language pathologist also joined them, bringing "frog juice" and "green frog dip." During the party the kids discussed what they had learned about the Bahamas. They did not have to ponder and strain: it came pouring out—a much different scenario than when they had to take a test in one of their content classes.

Christine was quite pleased with the study. It allowed her students to use skills that are a required part of any curriculum and of their IEP. She watched their oral and written language blossom. In fact, Christine considers the learner-centered approach a "miraculous" tool that unlocked her students' hidden abilities.

IN CLOSING

The idea of "whole" language lends itself to a broad-based view of literacy. For most of us, literacy is the use of an alphabetic code; for others visual arts, music, drama, or dance may be the vehicle of communication.

Whole language teachers want to create an environment that allows learners to explore and expand their mode or modes of literacy; to become independent and self-directed. Letting go, allowing learners to take control of their learning, is not an easy task for teachers—especially those who are used to structuring and cushioning their students' curriculum. As teachers have discovered, however, letting go comes easier through literature study groups, workshops, and learner-centered studies. These formats encourage learners to become self-directed with the help of teacher support that guides but doesn't get in the way. They give teachers something to "hang on" to as their students learn how to learn with a safety net. As the students and teachers become more confident, the safety net becomes less and less necessary.

Moving Toward an Inclusive Environment

If you are thinking about changing to a more learner-centered curriculum, or even if you are already in the process of doing so, parents, other special educators, general education teachers, principals, and counselors should become participants. They need not be active participants, but they should at least be informed about what is going on in your classroom.

Why does it matter that you share your beliefs and successes with those who will listen? First, it is one way to change perceptions about what "special" learners can accomplish. Second, it supports the idea of inclusive educational environments. Inclusive environments start by changing attitudes. An inclusive educational community is not one in which some learners are segregated from the mainstream because the mainstream isn't designed for real diversity. An inclusive educational community truly accepts all learners and values their diversity. Individual teachers can do a great deal to change attitudes by informing, seeking suggestions from other stakeholders, spreading the good news, and collaborating.

INFORM

Tell parents, colleagues, administrators, and support staff about your curriculum. Share your goals. The building principal may not be aware of the amount of reading and writing and research that goes on in your classroom. Schedule a short conference with your principal and other relevant administrators to talk about your vision and your plans for accomplishing your goals. These people are in a position to help you. I once explained to my principal that because I had to teach certain subjects that were required for high school graduation, I had less formal scheduled time for reading and written language development with my hearing-impaired students. I therefore planned to infuse the content areas with reading and writing. Reading and writing would be my main goals but within the context of geography, science, and so on. I lamented that $75, my annual allotment from the special education budget, was not enough to purchase some good reading materials I had discovered. To my surprise, the principal told me that if I would give him a list of the books I wanted, he would order them for me.

I also discovered that it was to my benefit to share what we were doing in my class with my colleagues. At first I was oblivious to my coworker's perceptions of special education classrooms. But when I gave my film orders to the media librarian, she often suggested that I take a box of plastic letters to my class—they were in a mess and my students might enjoy sorting them. I usually responded, "No, we really don't have time to do that." It finally occurred to me that she really had no idea about what went on in my classroom. So one day I started telling her about all the things we did—things we read, writing projects, and units of study. After that, she began asking what we were studying, and within a few days, she brought me all kinds of information and ideas. She became my best resource and supporter.

Some teachers have found that including an article about their classroom activities in the school newspaper or simply mounting writing projects or displaying art projects in the hall are wonderful ways to advertise to the school community. In this way everybody, including students, can be informed about what happens in your room. Don't keep it a secret! For the first issue of her school's newspaper, Pam Evans submitted the following announcement:

Adventurers in Room 19 will be on the trail of LEARNING! Adventures in Reading, Writing, Thinking, Speaking, and Listening will include lots of experiential, hands-on activities that will allow students to develop strategies and skills for a lifetime of learning. Emphasis will be on action, responsibility and cooperation.

Not only do you need to advertise within the school building, you also need to inform parents about what you are doing. Many teachers write parents a letter explaining curriculum expectations. A similar letter to classroom teachers is also a good idea, especially if you provide resource services. Here is a sample:

Dear Parents:
This year I am trying a new approach to learning in my classroom. I will be developing a whole language learning environment, and I want to tell you what it will involve. First I'll outline the basic philosophy of whole language:

- All children can develop literacy skills.
- Just as children are immersed in spoken language during oral language development, they should be immersed in print during written language development.
- Children learn to read and write when they are engaged in activities that are meaningful to them.
- Errors are markers of growth.
- Each individual's culture, experience, knowledge, and skills deserve respect.
- Each learner has his or her own starting point and rate of growth.

In my classroom I will put these beliefs into practice by reading to the children every day. They will also have opportunities each day to read individually. We will read story books, information books, magazines, and plays. The children will develop their reading skills through "real" reading. During the process, I will support them and demonstrate reading skills to help them become more fluent and independent readers. My goal is to help each student become a lifelong reader.

We will also write every day. The students will write in journals, write reports, letters, and write books. The students will work on organization, punctuation, capitalization, spelling, and other writing skills while they are actually writing. They will not use skills worksheets. In addition, we will not have a weekly spelling test because students will be working toward their own personal spelling goals.

To organize our learning I will use thematic units. The children will choose themes that interest them. For example, if the students want to study space we will read all kinds of books and stories, fiction and nonfiction, related to the topic. They will research questions of interest. For example, they might want to know about space exploration or manned flights.

We will be doing a lot of reading and writing and learning! I invite each of you to visit our class and become involved in the fun and excitement. Please call or stop by and I will be happy to answer any specific questions.

 Sincerely,

 Charlotte Keefe

Finally, don't be shy about contacting your local newspaper when there is a special event or speaker in your class. Of course, you should get parental permission before any photographs are printed in the newspaper, but it's worth the effort. Kids love to see their pictures in the paper, and it sends a positive message about school to the community.

SEEK SUGGESTIONS

You may find that "advertising" presents a good opportunity to seek suggestions. While you are discussing your plans with administrators, for example, you may want to find out the exact curriculum mandates. Often the guidelines for specific grade-level curriculum are not specific about how skills and content should be covered, and you and your administrator can discuss how you might accomplish grade objectives in the context of your whole language approach. Likewise, it is a good idea to discuss IEP objectives with special education personnel. Again, you will find that it is not difficult to address these objectives in a whole language curriculum. When you involve your supervisors in the process, they can more confidently support your efforts.

In the same vein, soliciting ideas from mainstream teachers may be a first step toward including your students in their classroom. One special education teacher asked a social studies teacher for help on a Native American theme unit. She was a little apprehensive, because the social studies teacher had not been very complimentary about the special education program in the past. However, after they had talked awhile, the social studies teacher invited the students in the special education class to join her class because they were also studying Native Americans. It has been my experience that seeking assistance from others often results in a productive collaborative relationship, one you perhaps wouldn't expect.

SPREAD THE NEWS

After you advertise your plans and seek suggestions, it is important to communicate your students' successes no matter how small. One teacher I know thinks nothing of insisting that the principal drop everything and come to her room to see what her children have done. Her exceptional enthusiasm has paid off because the entire school community knows that her students are readers and writers and that they are learning things they never thought possible.

Pulling people into your classroom may not be your style of spreading the news; however, you can certainly spread it through the school newspaper, a class newsletter, and even a "good news" phone call to parents.

COLLABORATE

There are many educators, in both general and special education, who use the learner-centered philosophy to guide their curriculum and shape their attitudes toward learners. These individuals should seek each other out for support and collaboration. A teacher in general education may want some ideas about how to support a learner who has difficulty and diverse needs; a special education teacher may be interested in including his or her students in mainstream education. In reality, both are interested in the same thing: How can I create the best learning environment possible for all learners? Collaboration can focus on creating an inclusive environment, the role the special educator can play in the general education classroom, and how to expand the curriculum to include all learners.

Brainstorm ways to achieve an inclusive environment
- Compare the learning goals of mainstream and "special" students. Shared goals (literacy, social skills, career education, and life skills).
- Peer tutoring and "buddy" learning.
- Cooperative learning groups.
- Cooperative activities (cooking, art, games).
- Learning centers that are multi-level.
- Units of study that allow learners to work at their own level.

Role of the special educator in the classroom
- As co-teacher rather than an assistant, co-plans activities.
- Provides mini-lessons and demonstrations to any learner who needs extra support.
- Locates resources and materials.
- Takes an active role in evaluation of all learners

EXPANDING THE CURRICULUM

We usually think about adapting the curriculum for special learners, but I prefer to expand or stretch the curriculum for inclusion. Because learner-centered curriculum is a basic tenet of a whole language philosophy, it may only take a little creative thinking to discover how learners with mild, moderate, and severe disabilities can benefit from being included in a general education classroom. For example, students with severe disabilities need to develop skills in the areas of work, socialization, life skills, recreation, and community living. General education includes these same goals. Once you have identified these similarities, how the objectives on an IEP can be addressed becomes clearer. In one class, for example, while other students were engaged in writing, a student with severe disabilities created a shopping list from pictures cut out of a magazine.

For learners with mild to moderate disabilities, classroom activities need not be drastically changed. Theme studies allow learners to learn and demonstrate knowledge at their own level, rather than demanding that they meet preconceived expectations. Learners who have less advanced skills are not penalized; they are able to be successful and included with their age peers.

I once observed a second-grade whole language classroom in which two children with learning disabilities were totally included for the first time. The resource teacher provided the classroom teacher with information about their strengths and monitored their progress quite closely. I did not know which children were being "included" until they were pointed out. I asked the teacher if she did anything differently or changed the curriculum. Because she used a learner-centered approach, she did not have the same expectations for all the students, but all were engaged in basically the same activities at some level. While the other students were engaged in independent work, she would often work with these two students individually. She also complimented the resource teacher for making her aware of alternative ways for these students to demonstrate their knowledge, allowing them to draw pictures or retell a story orally, for example, if they were unable to express themselves adequately through writing. This teacher had learned to expand her definition of literacy.

Of course, there should also be a collaborative relationship with parents. Most parents want to help their children. Some feel more prepared than others; some want to but feel they simply can't. It is important to involve parents as much as possible, even those who feel they have nothing to offer. Every year Barb Kinsella sends a letter inviting the parents of her students to participate in classroom activities—as helpers, as resource providers, as tutors, as guest speakers, and so on. Her intent is to be as open and flexible as possible so that all parents can participate. But sometimes there are a few parents who do not feel they have anything to offer. One year as Barb was discussing with the class how their parents would be participating in class, one of her students said he wanted his mother to come to school and cook hamburgers. "She cooks real good hamburgers," he said. His mother had not volunteered to participate so Barb thought this might be a good way to involve her. At first, the mother was a little hesitant, but after Barb explained how much her son wanted her to come, she agreed. Together they planned how they would do the cooking. The hamburger meal was a great success. In fact, the mother volunteered to come to school as a helper.

In addition to working in the classroom, parents are often eager to know how they can help at home. For some families, however, traditional homework assignments are a source of frustration, and the stress they cause far outweighs any conceivable benefits. But there are alternative "homework" activities that can have tremendous benefits while avoiding stressful situations. For example, a parent reading *with* a child can encourage a positive interaction. What is important, however, is that parents create a risk-free, supportive situation for their child rather than one that sets the child up for failure.

Margaret Glass encourages all the parents to attend the fall open house at her school. She takes this opportunity to brag about students' accomplishments. Then she tells parents how they can be active participants in their child's reading program. She explains in detail how to do "shared reading"—reading the child's "homework" book aloud once as the child listens; reading with the child; and listening while the child reads solo. Parents who are unable to attend receive a letter with a written explanation of the process. Sending a homework book home every night, Margaret believes, has really boosted her reading program.

The following tips will encourage parents to read with their child:

- Support and encourage your child's reading just as you supported learning when he or she was beginning to walk and talk.
- Read aloud to your child on a regular basis. Make it an intimate situation—let your child sit on your lap, or very close to you, with your arm around him or her. (If some of your students have parents who can't read, send home read-along tapes with a recorder. Suggest that the parents and child listen and follow along together.)
- Invite your child to read along with you. Make it a low-risk situation with this procedure:

    Let your child choose a book. Discuss the title and picture on the cover and what the book might be about. Encourage your child to make predictions if the book is not one you have previously read. Read the book to your child and feel free to discuss events that occur. Next, invite your child to read the book with you for a second reading. (When you feel it is appropriate, let your child read a word or phrase that is predictable without your support.) Then encourage your child to read through the book alone and give the child generous praise. If the child does not feel confident enough to read through the book alone, try "echo" reading: read a sentence or two and have the child echo what you read.

    During your child's reading, he or she might substitute a word that is not exactly the same as the one in the text but makes sense. When this happens, don't stop the reading to correct! At other times your child may come to an unknown word or substitute a word that doesn't make sense. Again, exercise some patience. Give your child the opportunity to figure out the correct word by prompting him or her to continue reading. Chances are that he or she will try to make sense out of what was read. If the child gets tangled up or does not self-correct, at the end of the sentence you might gently ask, "Did that make sense to you? What word would make sense?" However, if the child becomes frustrated, simply provide the word and let the reading continue. Avoid criticism or advice.

Here are additional activities to do with your child:

Ideas for "homework":
- Each night at dinner have the child share one fact learned that day.
- When driving, have your child help you with navigation. Have him or her read maps, road signs, and billboards.
- Let your child write shopping lists for weekly menus, special occasions, or just a run to the store.
- Encourage your child to keep a daily journal.
- When is your child's birthday? Have him or her read about games and activities that make up a good party and write up a plan for a birthday party.
- Co-author an autobiography of the child with your child. You write half from your perspective, and your child writes half from his or her perspective.
- When you make grocery lists, let your child sort coupons for the items on the lists.
- Invite your child to write letters to favorite movie stars or athletes.
- Cooking and baking activities are great. Share the recipe reading and measuring as well as the clean up.
- Let children make their own math problems from seeds, rocks, shells, legos, or whatever else you have.
- Invite your child to make books out of things he or she can read in the environment (such as candy wrappers, logos from advertisements).
- Let your child make greeting cards for special occasions.
- After reading a story, encourage children to write a story similar to it or try a different ending.

For older children:
- Have your child identify one or two interesting jobs and then investigate salary, job qualifications, what the job involves, and future prospects.
- Invite your child to research the cost of owning and maintaining a car.
- Involve your child in planning family meals for a week.
- Watch a TV documentary as a family and ask your child to write a summary of the program. You might ask your child such questions as, What were the issues involved? Did the coverage seem fair? What was the significance of the event?
- If your child is disgruntled about school rules, invite him or her to rewrite the school dress code, attendance rules, and discipline code.
- Read and discuss newspaper and magazine articles.
- Sunday newspapers, comic sections, and advertisement sections are an excellent source for learning and applying "life skills." Let your child talk about items on his or her wish list. Talk about pricing. How much money is $19.99? How much money do you have? How much money do you need to get everything you want?

- Have older children read to a younger brother or sister. This will help you out when you have stressful moments.

Whole family activities:
- Read a book together as a family. Keep a chart of how many pages the family reads each week.
- Write letters as a family; each member contributes a section. Make audio or videotapes to accompany the letter.
- Plan a reading dinner; everyone brings a book to the table to read while eating.
- Plan a family field trip. Share experiences in conversation or writing.
- Organize a family literature group. Discuss what everyone is reading. Share what you liked and didn't like, how you felt about what you read, whether your feelings changed.
- Open and sort junk mail with your children. Talk about why you consider it "junk."
- Have a family mailbox where family members can exchange notes and messages.
- Play cards and board games and teach children how to keep score.

Long-term activities:
- Subscribe to an age-appropriate children's magazine. Encourage your child to enter the contests or send away for the free offers mentioned in the magazine.
- Give your child an allowance and explain how to budget.
- Show your child how to order an item from a catalog using money he or she has saved.
- Designate an area for artistic work. Provide your child with art materials, such as paints, paper, markers, and glue. Talk about artwork creations and encourage the child to write about them.
- Encourage children to develop hobbies or craft skills. Besides learning a leisure activity, they practice important skills.
- Have children "publish" a family newspaper to keep up with family activities.
- Learning keyboarding has helped some children improve their reading skills. Encourage children to use a word-processor if you have one.

Hints to encourage reading and writing:
- Encourage children to listen to tapes of story-tellers and books on tape. Check your local library's tape collection.
- Provide a variety of reading materials for your child. Browse at garage sales and library book sales for children's books.
- Talk about the characteristics of things (shape, color, size, etc.) with your child.
- Have your child draw pictures of stories you have read together or favorite parts of a story.
- Praise your child's efforts at reading, writing, and other literacy activities.
- Provide your child with appropriate writing materials (paper, pens, pen-

cils, markers). Try to keep these items together in one area so that they are easy to find.

- Don't worry about spelling, punctuation, or other errors, on the first draft of a child's written piece.
- Help your child through the editing process, but let him or her lead you—don't push.
- Keep your child's writing in a folder. It's fun to go back and see how much progress the child has made.

Summer activities:

- Brainstorm a list of fun activities for the summer with your child. Write dates on the calendar.
- Take a trip to the library. Help your child select books.
- Suggest writing to a pen pal (teachers can pass on the names of classmates who have asked to be pen pals).
- Special days in June are Flag Day and Father's Day. Invite your child to read about our national flag. Design a Father's Day card.
- Go on a walk with your child. Look for insects and observe what they are doing.
- Read the comics together.
- Invite your child to help in the kitchen—planning meals, baking cookies.
- Invite your child to cut out pictures of favorite foods from magazines.
- Make a weather chart together. Keep a daily record of the weather.
- Invite your child to send a postcard to a grandparent, aunt, or uncle.
- Help your child start an inventory list of toys.
- Visit the zoo. Read about the animals.
- Invite your child to make a map of the neighborhood.
- Suggest inviting two friends for lunch. Plan the menu and shop for groceries together.
- Invite your child to start a summer journal and write something every day.
- Independence Day is July 4. Read about America's independence. Plan a Fourth of July celebration together.
- Help your child start a photo album of family members.
- Plan a vacation together. Invite your child to write to the chamber of commerce of various places to visit to get information.
- Suggest producing a neighborhood play.
- In general, talk and listen, read, play games, share hobbies, news, TV programs, and special events.

In addition, you can suggest low-stress "homework" activities, long-term projects, family projects, and summer activities.

LET'S DO IT TOGETHER

Educators in general and those who work in special education have a lot to offer each other. In the same way, parents and members of the community can also provide support and resources that will assist us tremendously in attaining quality education for all our learners.

The underlying idea of the whole language philosophy is to keep learning *whole,* and this idea can certainly be generalized to the learning community. Neither students nor teachers should be isolated or sheltered in a subcommunity where they will miss out on learning opportunities or encounter an unnecessary duplication of services and resources. When the greater learning community is aware of educational goals, when they are aware of successes, and when they have an opportunity to be a part of these successes, attitudes about "special" learners will surely change. All children can learn.

FIFTEEN

The Evolution of a Resource Teacher

Research has allowed educators to validate their intuition. It has also been a source of exciting new ideas and inspired teachers with enough confidence to move from intuition to active change (see Appendix).

Maria Allen is one example of a teacher who wanted to change her teaching. She had been a resource teacher for seven years, but she was dissatisfied with the progress the fourth-, fifth-, and sixth-grade students who were identified as learning disabled were making. These students spent anywhere from thirty minutes to two hours in her classroom every day. For the most part, the goals on their IEPs reflected their deficiencies—in reading, writing, spelling, and sometimes in math and social skills. The reading skills of the two-hour students were so poor, they could not make passing grades in a content area such as social studies or science. Maria's role had thus become one of tutor or support for the skills program in the general education classes.

Maria decided to rethink her role as a special education teacher. She took a year's leave of absence from teaching to work on her master's degree and revitalize her thinking. This hiatus eventually led her to explore a whole language philosophy and to engage in her own personal soul-searching about how she might apply it in her resource room. The whole language approach matched what she had intuitively believed about the learning environment her students needed, and she began to investigate how she might introduce it into her teaching. She identified three major concerns: (1) the varying length of time students spent in her class; (2) the contrast between a whole language approach and the skills-centered general education classes; and (3) the students' IEP goals, which emphasized specific skills. She concluded that she should organize the class in terms of the amount of scheduled time students spent in her classroom. As for the other two concerns, she predicted that students would achieve the IEP goals and be able to adjust to a different learning environment.

After reading a great deal and observing in whole language classrooms, Maria decided to introduce literature circles, a writing workshop, thematic units of study, and activity centers. During literature circles and workshops she would present mini-lessons as needed. During theme studies she planned to

156

encourage students to use strategies such as KWLS and semantic mapping to focus their research. Their daily work in the resource room would include researching topics, recording their discoveries, creating displays, and producing a final presentation. In addition, she would set up ongoing centers in writing, reading, math, and art, as well as temporary centers that would reflect current study topics. These centers would allow independence and individual instruction. Maria's ultimate goal was to encourage her students to become active learners engaged in authentic, purposeful activities.

But what about general class assignments? When would there be time to work with students on these? She decided to set aside the last twenty minutes of the school day so that students could come in if they needed extra help.

THE NEW SCHEDULE

Maria now had a good idea of how she would organize her program for thirty-minute students, one-hour students, and two-hour students.

Thirty-Minute Students

Literature Study Group

Monday-Thursday: 15–20 minutes   Read silently or with a buddy or follow along with a tape.
10 minutes   Write in response journal or participate in oral discussion with group depending on schedule designed by group.
Friday: Center time/individual conferences/mini-lessons.

Theme Study

Resource time spent on reading, researching, and group work.
Center time/individual conferences/mini-lessons integrated into theme study.

Reading Aloud

One-Hour Students

15–20 minutes   Journal writing/center time.
20 minutes   Read silently or with a buddy or follow along with a tape.
10 minutes   Group discussion.
5–10 minutes   Reading response.

Two-Hour Students

First Hour

15–20 minutes   Journal writing/center time.
20 minutes   Read silently or with a buddy or follow along with tape.

10 minutes   Group discussion.
5–10 minutes   Reading response.

Second Hour

15–20 minutes   Teacher demonstration.
20–30 minutes   Cooperative groups or independent work.
10–15 minutes   Group or independent student-teacher conferences or whole class discussions.

Although Maria felt she had built a solid foundation in whole language practice and developed a good plan, she was still a bit leery about actually pulling it off. She wondered what the teachers in the general education classes would say, since she had always reinforced their curriculum. Now she was planning to shed the role of well-paid tutor. She had to admit it sounded somewhat radical. As she talked about her ideas with other special educators, someone suggested that it was time to "redefine" her job.

To begin putting together her new job description, Maria searched for the district's job description of her job. What she found was a list of rather vague job competencies. But there was no mandated philosophical approach, so she saw the vagueness as a plus. Then she asked herself, "What does a special education teacher *need* to be?" The obvious answer was *"special!"* Special means different, distinct, distinguished, or individual. Maria realized that her resource room in the past had not been special, it had merely been a rehash of the general education classes. She was determined that her special education classroom would be different. It would be an environment that allowed her students to express their individual strengths, and it would support their learning through learner-centered activities, not a predetermined curriculum that was in no way tailored to their individual needs. She would implement what she had learned about responsive assessment using portfolios, running records, anecdotal records, and student self-evaluations. IEP goals would be authentic goals: students would write, read, become independent learners and problem solvers, and work cooperatively and collaboratively with others.

Maria was excited and confident about her plans as she started off the year. Her scheduling gave her a useful structure for redesigning her classroom. She soon discovered, however, that although her time schedules were a good place to start, strict adherence to them was impossible if she really wanted her students to become independent learners. Mason, for example, found a play in a student magazine and asked if the class could read it aloud. The students really liked it and wanted to dramatize it. This caused great excitement and a flurry of activity. Quickly they organized a production schedule. Their first job was to make scenery. Within a few days they had accumulated enough large boxes to construct scenery that would stand alone. They chose a director and assigned parts. Next they gathered props. Then, of course, there was rehearsal time. Most students memorized their parts, but a few had some difficulty. The solution was to make cue cards that they could refer to when necessary. When everything was ready, they expected to have a real production and sent invitations to various classes. As the year progressed, what Maria discovered was that deviating from the schedule became the rule rather than the exception. After the initial play production, her students began writing their own plays and even produced a musical.

There were times when Maria felt that she had lost control (which she had, because the students were taking responsibility for their own learning). When she questioned herself about what was occurring in her classroom, she checked the IEP goals and her informal evaluations. What were the students learning? They were reading, writing, and spelling, in fact, better than ever. Their skills were improving without drill sheets. Why were they improving? They were reading and writing, yes but now they were doing it for themselves.

Maria was pleased with the progress her students made. The next fall she was given the title "inclusion" teacher as well as resource teacher. During the year her resource room maintained the basic elements of the previous year, but for one hour each day she worked as co-teacher in Helen Livingston's fourth-grade classroom. It had been very rewarding for Maria because she felt that she had been able to influence Helen to move toward a more learner-centered curriculum. She did this by demonstrating that literature circles and workshops can be used with learners at different ability levels. Helen began to see that she didn't need different lesson plans for the special education students.

A new academic year is approaching and Maria is again redefining her job and her responsibilites. She is planning to work with the fifth-grade teacher just as she worked with Helen. In the meantime, Helen has attended many whole language workshops and feels confident about including special students in her classroom. She wants all her students to begin and end the day in her class so they will feel that they are members, but she still believes Maria's resource class is necessary for extra support. Maria learned a great deal from working with Helen, and while she is not sure where special education is heading, she believes that "inclusion" is most successful when the general education classroom is learner-centered. For Maria, the real beauty of the whole language philosophy is the fundamental principle that all children can learn—without being labeled—because they are allowed to grow into literacy at a comfortable rate that gives them the confidence to attain some degree of competency. As educators, we want to accept and celebrate all children's accomplishments and praise them for their efforts.

Summary of Selected Research

• **Research supports literature-based reading instruction over basal readers and mastery learning instruction.**

Numerous studies, which have involved academic underachievers, limited English speakers, and "stalled readers" (those who have made no progress in reading for more than one year), indicate greater success with literature-based reading instruction (Tunnell and Jacobs 1989)

• **Whole language does not retard understanding of phonics or vocabulary development.**

Lee Gunderson and Jon Shapiro (1988) conducted a year-long study involving fifty-two students in two first-grade classrooms in Richmond, British Columbia. Their study revealed that students in a whole language environment understood phonics, which was evident in the phonics generalization in their spelling, and did not miss out on high-frequency vocabulary. The low-frequency vocabulary, however, did differ from that in basal readers because in the whole language environment, the low-frequency vocabulary was more current and reflective of student interests.

• **Learners in whole language classrooms do not necessarily perform worse than students in traditional classrooms on standardized tests. They may in fact do better on awareness of problem-solving strategies.**

A study by Carol Stice and Nancy Bertrand (1989) provided evidence that "at-risk" children in whole language classrooms performed as well or better on the Stanford Achievement Test and on writing tasks than their matches in traditional classrooms. While there was no difference on quantitative writing measures, such as number of words, number of T-units, and number of sentences, the retelling scores of students in whole language classrooms were higher. These students retold longer and more complete versions of stories. They also had a greater awareness of alternative strategies for dealing with problems, they appeared to feel better about themselves as readers and writers, and they exhibited more independence.

- **Whole language instruction helps learners with disabilities become engaged readers who read more and have a better attitude toward reading.**

Kelly Oberlin and Sherrie Shugarman (1989) conducted a study involving fourteen students with learning disabilities who were instructed in a reading workshop format. Pre- and posttest measures indicated improved reading attitude and level of book involvement. Observations of positive attitudes were validated through students' comments in their dialogue journals. In addition, students participated willingly, acquired books for their own personal libraries, and increased their use of the school library. The average number of books read by each student increased from one per year to twenty per year.

- **Whole language helps students take responsibility for their learning.**

Jo Beth Allen, Barbara Micholove, Betty Shockley, and Marsha West (1991, 1993) looked at the effectiveness of whole language instruction in one school. Their most convincing evidence was the story of Joseph, a one-time bully who not only became more literate, a classroom leader, and an engaged learner, but most remarkable of all, took himself out of special education. He quietly refused to go to the resource room for students identified as mentally retarded and behaviorally disordered. He felt he didn't fit. Apparently he was right, because according to the most recent evaluation, he was "cured" of mental retardation. His teachers feel that whole language experiences, time, choice, supported risk taking and belonging have made a difference. As his good friend Cory observed, "He got smart fast."

- **Whole language is effective with learners who have hearing impairments.**

A year-long study of whole language in one classroom involved deaf high school students who read six to seven years below grade level. After a period of whole language instruction, students' independent reading levels increased between one and three grade levels, and in interviews they indicated a more positive attitude toward reading and writing. In addition, their grammatical fluency in writing also increased (Schleper and Farmer 1991).

- **Learners with disabilities in whole language classrooms are strategic learners.**

In my own research, my colleagues and I studied a primary (6–8 year-olds) whole language classroom for students identified as learning disabled and mentally retarded (Keefe, Andrews-Beck, and Davis 1995). We analyzed the behaviors associated with writing while the students were actually engaged in the writing process. What we discovered is that they used numerous strategies, which we categorized as metacognitive, seeking external help, and relying on oneself. Observed strategies classified as metacognitive included verbal rehearsal, rereading, use of prior knowledge, and questioning. Seeking external sources of help included the use of the dictionary, environmental print, books, pictures, teacher and peer assistance, and previous writing. Strategies that revealed independence included invented spelling, correction without prompting, composing without help, internalization of conventions, helping others, and persistence in desire to write. Documenting these strategies was particularly significant because learners identified as mildly/moderately disabled are often characterized as strategy deficient and dependent.

• Holistic instruction contributes to phonemic awareness.

Pamela J. Winsor and David P. Pearson (1992) conducted a study in which they analyzed the development of phonemic awareness among first-grade children with average intelligence considered to be at risk. The classroom teacher used a holistic instructional approach (literature-based opportunities for writing; little, if any, explicit phonics instruction). Data sources and analyses included observations, individual assessment of phonemic awareness, teacher interviews, child interviews, and parent questionnaires. The researchers drew four conclusions: (1) children who are at risk for failure to read and write and are engaged in holistic instructional programs improve their performance on tasks of phonemic awareness; (2) phonemic awareness is necessary but not sufficient for reading and writing success; (3) use of invented spelling, and choral and independent reading of predictable texts contribute to phonemic awareness. Holistic instruction contributes to phonemic awareness but does not guarantee reading success for all children; and (4) home literacy contributes to phonemic awareness.

• Whole language instructional strategies are effective with at-risk students.

Paul R. Hoffman and Janet A. Norris (1994) conducted a study of kindergarten students in an inner-city school in which 92 percent of the children were considered at risk because of low SES, and 75 percent of the children qualified for the Chapter I reading program. To compare a whole language curriculum with an alphabet-based curriculum the researchers chose twenty students in four different classrooms. The whole language curriculum was structured around indirect, literature-based exploration of print and reading, while the alphabet-based curriculum was based on the systematic and explicit teaching of a single letter of the alphabet each week. The effectiveness of the two curriculums was measured by pre- and posttest scores of the Test of Early Reading Ability-2 (Reid, Hresko, Hammill 1989), which focuses on reading development in the areas of meaning, alphabet, and conventions. The children in the whole language group made more gains than the children in the alphabet-based curriculum in all these areas; the difference in gains was only significant for the meaning subtest. The authors concluded that since children learned alphabetic knowledge within meaningful reading experiences, teaching it separately, outside a meaningful context, may not be the most efficient use of limited classroom time.

References

Children's literature resources

Adoption

Bunin, C., and S. Bunin. 1976. *Is That Your Sister?* New York: Pantheon.
Gordon, S. 1980. *The Boy Who Wanted a Family.* New York: HarperCollins.
Krementz, J. 1982. *How It Feels to Be Adopted.* New York: Knopf.

Anorexia Nervosa

Dean, K. S. 1980. *Maggie Adams, Dancer.* New York: Avon.
Levenkron, S. 1978. *The Best Little Girl in the World.* New York: Warner.

Anxiety

Giff, P. R. 1990. *Today Was a Terrible Day.* New York: Penguin.
Howe, J. 1986. *My First Days of School.* Julian Messner.
Josse, B. 1991. *Mama, Do You Love Me?* San Francisco: Chronicle Books.
Kantrowitz, M. 1976. *Willy Bear.* New York: Parents' Magazine Press.
Soderstrom, M. 1981. *Maybe Tomorrow I'll Have a Good Time.* New York: Human Sciences Press.

Behavior

Aardema, V. 1975. *Why Mosquitos Buzz in People's Ears.* New York: Dial.
Blume, J. 1974. *Blubber.* New York: Dell.
Burch, R. 1966. *Queenie Peavy.* New York: Dell.
Munsch, R. 1985. *Thomas' Snowsuit.* Willowdale, ONT: Annick Press.
Wilhelm, H. 1986. *Let's Be Friends Again!* New York: Crown.

Child Abuse and Safety

Garden, N. 1991. *Lark in the Morning.* New York: Farrar, Straus, Giroux.
Howard, E. 1986. *Gillyflower.* New York: Atheneum.
Levin, B. 1992. *Mercy's Mill.* New York: Greenwillow.

Nelson, T. 1992. *The Beggar's Ride*. New York: Orchard.
Wolverton, L. 1987. *Running Before the Wind*. Boston: Houghton Mifflin.

Death

Miska, C. S. 1971. *Annie and the Old One*. New York: Atlantic Monthly.
Rylant, C. 1992. *Missing May*. New York: Orchard Books.
Smith, D. B. 1973. *A Taste of Blackberries*. New York: Scholastic.
Warburg, S. S. 1969. *Growing Time*. Boston: Houghton Mifflin.

Family Relationships

Blume, J. 1972. *Tales of a Fourth Grade Nothing*. New York: Dell.
———. 1974. *The Pain and the Great One*. New York: Bantam Doubleday Dell.
———. 1980. *Superfudge*. New York: Dell.
Carlson, N. S. 1986. *The Family Under the Bridge*. New York: HarperCollins.
Cowley, J. 1988. *A Walk with Grandpa*. Shortland.
Gardener, J. R. 1983. *Stone Fox*. New York: HarperCollins.
Josse, B. M. 1991. *Mama, Do You Love Me?* San Francisco: Chronicle Books.
Kellog, S. 1976. *Much Bigger Than Martin*. New York: Bantam Doubleday Dell.
Mayer, G., and M. Mayer. 1992. *The New Potty*. Racine, WI: Western Publishing.
Munsch, R. 1990. *I'll Love You Forever*. Buffalo, NY: Firefly Books.
Rylant, C. 1985. *The Relatives Came*. New York: Bradbury.
Spinelli, J. 1990. *Maniac Magee*. New York: Scholastic.

Feelings

Aliki. 1984. *Feelings*. New York: Morrow.
Blume, J. 1974. *The Pain and the Great One*. New York: Bantam Doubleday Dell.
Bunting, E. 1990. *Our Sixth-Grade Sugar Babies*. New York: HarperCollins.
Carle, E. 1977. *The Grouchy Ladybug*. New York: Crowell.
Giff, P. R. 1989. *Stacy Says Good-bye*. New York: Dell.
———. 1990. *Today Was a Terrible Day*. New York: Penguin.
Kellog, S. 1976. *Much Bigger Than Martin*. New York: Bantam Doubleday Dell.
Mayer, M. 1983. *I Was So Mad*. Racine, WI: Western Publishing.
Munsch, R. 1985. *Thomas' Snowsuit*. Willowdale, ONT: Annick Press.
Viorst, J. 1976. *Alexander and the Terrible, Horrible, No Good, Very Bad Day*. New York: Macmillan.
Wilhelm, H. 1986. *Let's Be Friends Again!* New York: Crown.

Feeling Different or Left Out

Blume, J. 1974. *Blubber*. New York: Dell.
Byars, B. 1970. *The Summer of the Swans*. New York: Penguin.
Cohen, B. 1990. *Molly's Pilgrim*. New York: Bantam.
Estes, E. 1944. *The Hundred Dresses*. New York: Scholastic.
Levine, H. 1989. *I Hate English*. New York: Scholastic.

Foster Care

Adler, C. 1981. *The Cat That Was Left Behind*. Boston: Houghton Mifflin.
Hansen, J. 1980. *The Gift-Giver*. Boston: Houghton Mifflin.
Myers, W. D. 1982. *Won't Know 'Til I Get There*. New York: Penguin.

Friendship

Blume, J. 1974. *Blubber*. New York: Dell.
Fleischman, S. 1986. *The Whipping Boy*. New York: Greenwillow.
Kellogg, S. 1986. *Best Friends*. New York: Bantam Doubleday Dell.
Kline, S. 1988. *Horrible Harry in Room 2B*. New York: Penguin.
Lobel, A. 1979. *Frog and Toad Are Friends*. New York: HarperCollins.
Silverstein, S. 1964. *The Giving Tree*. New York: HarperCollins.
Spinelli, J. 1990. *Maniac Magee*. New York: Scholastic.
Waber, B. 1975. *Ira Sleeps Over*. Boston: Houghton Mifflin.

Growing Up/Independence

Hoffman, M., and C. Binch. 1991. *Amazing Grace*. New York: Dial.
Kraus, R. 1971. *Leo the Late Bloomer*. Glen Burnie, MD: Windmill Press.
Munsch, R. 1990. *I'll Love You Forever*. Buffalo, NY: Firefly Books.
Silverstein, S. 1964. *The Giving Tree*. New York: HarperCollins.

Valuing Diversity

Bunting, E. 1991. *Fly Away Home*. Boston: Houghton Mifflin.
Byars, B. 1970. *The Summer of the Swans*. New York: Penguin.
Cohen, B. 1990. *Molly's Pilgrim*. New York: Bantam.
Lynne, C. 1990. *The Great Kapok Tree: A Tale of the Amazon Rain Forest*. San Diego: Harcourt Brace.
Robinson, B. 1972. *The Best Christmas Pageant Ever*. New York: HarperCollins.
Rohmer, H., and M. Anchondo. 1988. *How We Came to the Fifth World: Como Vinimos al Quinto Mundo*. Emeryville, CA: Children's Book Press.
Tolstoy, A. 1989. *The Great Big Enormous Turnip*. Boston: Houghton Mifflin.

Professional References

Allen, J. B., B. Micholove, and B. Shockley. 1993. *Engaging Children: Community and Chaos in the Lives of Young Literacy Learners*. Portsmouth, NH: Heinemann.
Allen, J. B., B. Micholove, B. Shockley, and M. West. 1991. "'I'm Really Worried About Joseph': Reducing the Risks of Literacy Learning." In *Reading Teacher*, 44, 7: 458–472.
Anderson, R. C., E. H. Hiebert, J. A. Scott, and I. Wilkinson. 1985. *Becoming a Nation of Readers*. Washington, DC: National Institute of Education.
Atwell, N. 1987. *In the Middle: Writing, Reading, and Learning with Adolescents*. Portsmouth, NH: Heinemann Boynton/Cook.
Beane, J. A., and M. W. Apple, eds. 1995. "The Case for Democratic Schools." In *Democratic Schools*. Alexandria, VA: Association for Supervision and Curriculum Development.
Beers, J. W., and E. H. Henderson. 1977. "A Study of Developing Orthographic Concepts Among First-Grade Children." In *Research in the Teaching of English*, 11: 133–148.
Bilken, D., with R. Bogdan, D. L. Ferguson, S. J. Searl, Jr., and S. J. Taylor. 1985. *Achieving the Complete School: Strategies for Effective Mainstreaming*. New York: Teachers College Press.

Bissex, G. L. 1980. *GNYS AT WRK: A Child Learns to Write and Read.* Cambridge, MA: Harvard University Press.

Calkins, L. M. 1984. *Lessons from a Child: On the Teaching and Learning of Writing.* Portsmouth, NH: Heinemann.

Calkins, L. M., with Shelley Harwayne. 1991. *Living Between the Lines.* Portsmouth, NH: Heinemann.

Cambourne, B. 1982. "How Do Learning Disabled Children Read?" In *Topics in Learning and Learning Disabilities,* 1: 59–67.

———. 1988. *The Whole Story.* New York: Scholastic.

Cartwright, G. P. 1968. "Written Language Abilities of Normal and Educable Mentally Retarded Children." In *American Journal of Mental Deficiency,* 72: 494–508.

Clay, M. 1985. *The Early Detection of Reading Difficulties.* 3d ed. Portsmouth, NH: Heinemann Boynton/Cook.

Coger, L. I., and M. R. White. 1967. *Readers' Theatre Handbook.* Glenview, IL: Scott, Foresman.

Council for Exceptional Children. 1993. "CEC Policy on Inclusive Schools and Community Settings." In *Supplement to Teaching Exceptional Children,* 25, 4.

Cowley, J. 1993. *Just This Once.* New York: Wright Group.

Cox, S., and L. Galda. 1990. "Multicultural Literature: Mirrors and Windows on a Global Community." In *Reading Teacher,* 4: 582–589.

Daniels, H. 1994. *Literature Circles: Voice and Choice in the Student-Centered Classroom.* York, ME: Stenhouse.

Demchak, M. A., and S. Drinkwater. 1992. "Preschoolers with Severe Disabilities: The Case Against Segregation." In *Topics in Early Childhood Special Education,* 11, 4: 70–83.

Doise, W., and G. Mugny. 1984. *The Social Development of the Individual.* New York: Pergamon.

Dudley-Marling, C. 1985. "Perceptions of the Usefulness of the IEP by Teachers of Learning Disabled and Emotionally Disturbed Children." In *Psychology in the Schools,* 22: 65–67.

Edelsky, C. 1991. "Authentic Reading/Writing Versus Reading/Writing Exercises." In *The Whole Language Catalog.* K. S. Goodman, Y. M. Goodman, and W. J. Hood, eds. Portsmouth, NH: Heinemann.

Elbow, P. 1973. *Writing Without Teachers.* New York: Oxford University Press.

Fisher, B. 1991. *Joyful Learning: Whole Language Kindergarten.* Portsmouth, NH: Heinemann.

Free and Inexpensive Stuff for Kids. Deephaven, MN: Meadowbrook.

Fuchs, D., and L. S. Fuchs. 1995. "Sometimes Separate is Better." In *Educational Leadership,* 52: 22–26.

Gentry, J. R. 1977. "A Study of the Orthographic Strategies of Beginning Readers." Ph.D. diss. University of Virginia, Charlottesville, VA.

———. 1982. "An Analysis of Developmental Spelling in GNYS AT WRK." In *Reading Teacher,* 36, 2: 192–200.

George, J. C. 1991. *My Side of the Mountain.* New York: Puffin.

Gerber, P. J., and K. B. Harris. 1983. "Using Juvenile Literature to Develop Social Skills in Learning Disabled Children." In *Pointer,* 27, 4: 29–32.

Goodman, K. 1968. *The Psycholinguistic Nature of the Reading Process.* Detroit, MI: Wayne State University Press.

———. 1969. "Analysis of Oral Reading Miscues: Applied Psycholinguistics." In *Reading Research Quarterly,* 5: 9–30.

————. 1986. *What's Whole in Whole Language?* Portsmouth, NH: Heinemann.

————. 1989. Preface. In *The Whole Language Evaluation Book.* K. S. Goodman, Y. M. Goodman, and W. J. Hood, eds. Portsmouth, NH: Heinemann.

Goodman, Y. 1985. "Kid Watching: Observing Children in the Classroom." In *Observing the Language Learner.* A. Jaggar and M. T. Smith-Burke, eds. Newark, DE: International Reading Association.

————. 1989. *Evaluation of Students: Evaluation of Teachers.*

Gunderson, L. 1995. *The Monday Morning Guide to Comprehension.* Markham, ONT: Pippin.

Gunderson, L., and J. Shapiro. 1988. "Some Findings on Whole Language Instruction." In *Reading-Canada-Lecture,* 5, 1: 22–26.

Graves, D. 1978. *Balance the Basics: Let Them Write.* New York: Ford Foundation.

————. 1983. *Writing: Teachers and Children at Work.* Portsmouth, NH: Heinemann.

————. 1994. *A Fresh Look at Writing.* Portsmouth, NH: Heinemann.

Halliday, M. A. K. 1978. *Language as Social Semiotic: The Social Interpretation of Language and Meaning.* Baltimore, MD: University Park Press.

Hansen, J. 1987. *When Writers Read.* Portsmouth, NH: Heinemann.

Harmin, M. 1993. *Strategies that Inspire Students: Instruction that Motivates both Excellence and Kindness.* Edwardsville, IL: The Strategy Project.

Harste, J. C., V. Woodward, and C. Burke. 1984. *Language Stories and Literacy Lessons.* Portsmouth, NH: Heinemann.

Harste, J. C., K. G. Short, and C. Burke. 1988. *Creating Classrooms for Authors: The Reading-Writing Connection.* Portsmouth, NH: Heinemann.

Henderson, E., and J. W. Beers. 1980. *Developmental and Cognitive Aspects of Learning to Spell.* Newark, DE: International Reading Association.

Heumann, J. E., and T. Hehr. 1994, Nov. 23. Communication to Chief State School Officers. Department of Education, Office of Special Education and Rehabilitation Service.

Hill, S., and T. Hill. 1990. *The Collaborative Classroom: A Guide to Cooperative Learning.* Portsmouth, NH: Heinemann.

Hobbs, N., ed. 1975. *Issues in the Classification of Children.* Vol. 2. San Francisco: Jossey-Bass.

Hoffman, P. R., and J. A. Norris. 1994. "Whole Language and Collaboration Work: Evidence from At-Risk Kindergarteners." In *Journal of Childhood Communication Disorders,* 16: 41–48.

Holdaway, D. 1979. *The Foundation of Literacy.* Portsmouth, NH: Heinemann.

Hollway, J. 1989. *Writing Dictionary.* Scarborough, ONT: Ginn Publishing Canada.

Hurray, G. 1987. *A Spelling Dictionary for Beginning Writers.* Cambridge, MA: Educators Publishing Service.

Inclusion Times. 1993, September. "It Means More Than Mainstreaming . . ." 1, 1: 2.

Irwin, P. A., and J. N. Mitchell. 1983. "A Procedure for Assessing the Richness of Retellings." In *Journal of Reading,* 26: 391–396.

Johns, J. 1991. "Literacy Portfolios: A Primer." In *Illinois Reading Council Journal,* 19, 3: 4–9.

Johnson, D., and R. Johnson. 1989. *Cooperation and Competition: Theory and Research.* Edina, MN: Interaction Book.

Johnson, D., G. Maruyama, R. Johnson, D. Nelson, and L. Skon. 1981. "Effects of Co-operative, Competitive and Individualistic Goal Structures on Achievement: A Meta-analysis." In *Psychological Bulletin,* 89: 47–62.

Johnston, P. 1992. *The Constructive Evaluation of Literate Activity.* White Plains, NY: Longman.

Kagan, S. 1985. *Cooperative Learning: Resources for Teachers.* Riverside, CA: University of California.

Keefe, C. H. 1992. "Developing Responsive IEPs Through Holistic Assessment." In *Intervention,* 28, 1: 34–40.

———. 1993. "Responsive Assessment for Special Learners." In *Journal of Reading and Writing Quarterly,* 9, 3: 215–226.

———. 1995. "Portfolios: Mirrors of Learning." In *Teaching Exceptional Children,* 27: 66–67.

———. (in press). "Literature Circles: Invitation to a Reading and Writing Community." In *LD Forum.*

Keefe, C. H., C. Andrews-Beck, and R. A. Davis. 1995. Manuscript submitted for publication. Observed writing behaviors of learners with mild disabilities in a whole language instructional environment.

Keefe, D. 1986. *My First Bike.* Mankata, MN: Baker Street Productions.

———. 1986. *What Do You Eat?* Mankato, MN: Baker Street Productions.

———. 1993. "The Keefe Inventory of Silent Reading: A Window into the Reading Process." In *Reading and Writing Quarterly: Overcoming Learning Difficulties,* 9, 3: 227–248.

Keegan, S., and K. Shrake. 1991. "Literature Study Groups: An Alternative to Ability Grouping." In *Reading Teacher,* 44, 8: 542–547.

King, D. 1982. "Interrelationships and Transactions: The Education of a Language User." Paper presented at IRA Impact Conference, Child Language Development, Columbia, MO.

Lamme, L. L., and C. Hysmith. 1991. "One School's Adventure into Portfolio Assessment." In *Language Arts,* 68: 629–640.

Lieberman, L. M. 1992. "Preserving Special Education . . . for Those Who Need It." In *Controversial Issues Confronting Special Education.* W. Stainback and S. Stainback, eds. Needham Heights, MA: Allyn & Bacon.

Lilly, M. S. 1986. "The Relationship Between General and Special Education: A New Face on an Old Issue." In *Counterpoint:* p. 10.

Lynch, E. C., and P. L. Beare. 1990. "The Quality of IEP Objectives and Their Relevance to Instruction for Students with Mental Retardation and Behavioral Disorders." In *Remedial and Special Education,* 11: 48–55.

Lynne, C. 1990. *The Great Kapok Tree.* San Diego: Harcourt Brace.

Manzo, A. V. 1969. "The Request Procedure." In *Journal of Reading,* 13, 2: 123–126.

Margolis, H., and L. A. Truesdell. 1987. "Do Special Education Teachers Use IEPs to Guide Instruction?" In *The Urban Review,* 19, 151–159.

Martin, E. W. 1994. "Inclusion: Rhetoric and Reality." In *Exceptional Parent:* 39–42.

Markwardt, F. C., Jr. 1989. *Peabody Individual Achievement Test-Revised.* Circle Pines, MN: American Guidance Service.

McGee, L. M., and D. J. Richgels. 1990. *Literacy Beginnings.* Needham Heights, MA: Allyn & Bacon.

Meir, D., and P. Schwarz. 1995. "The Hard Part Is Making It Happen." In *Democratiac Schools.* M. W. Apple and J. A. Beane, eds. Alexandria, VA: Association for Supervision and Curriculum Development.

Meyer, V., and D. Keefe. 1990. *Reading for Meaning: Selected Teaching Strategies.* Glenview, IL: Scott, Foresman.

Miller, D. 1993. "Teaching Adolescents with Behavioral/Emotional Disorders, Adolescent Offenders, and Adolescents At-Risk: A Literature-Based Approach." Paper presented at the 71st Annual Convention of the Council for Exceptional Children, San Antonio, TX.

Mooney, M. 1991. *Developing Life-Long Readers.* Willington, NZ: Learning Media, Ministry of Education.

Moran, M. R. 1987. "Options for Written Language Assessment." In *Focus on Exceptional Children,* 19, 5: 1–12.

Morrow, L. M. 1985. "Reading and Retelling Stories: Strategies for Emergent Readers." In *Reading Teacher,* 38, 9: 870–875.

National Association of State Boards of Education (NASBE) Study Group on Special Education. 1992. *Winners All: A Call for Inclusive Schools.* Alexandria, VA: NASBE.

Newman, J. 1985. "Insights from Recent Reading and Writing Research and Their Implications for Developing Whole Language Curriculum." In *Whole Language: Theory in Use.* J. Newman, ed. Portsmouth, NH: Heinemann.

New Zealand Ministry of Education. 1992. *Dancing with the Pen.* Distributed by Richard C. Owen Publishers, Katonah, NY.

Oberlin, K. J., and S. L. Shugarman. 1989. "Implementing the Reading Workshop with Middle School LD Readers." In *Journal of Reading,* 32, 8: 682–687.

Ogle, D. 1986. "K-W-L: A Teaching Model that Develops Active Reading of Expository Text." In *Reading Teacher,* 39, 6: 564–570.

O'Neil, J. 1993. "'Inclusive Education Gains Adherents." In *ASCD Update,* 35, 9: 1–5.

Palinscar, A. S., and A. L. Brown. 1984. "Reciprocal Teaching of Comprehension Fostering and Monitoring Activities." In *Cognition and Instruction,* 1: 117–175.

———. 1986. "Interactive Teaching to Promote Independent Reading from Text." In *Reading Teacher,* 39, 8: 771–777.

Parkes, B. 1986. *Who's In The Shed?* Crystal Lake, IL: Rigby Education.

Poplin, M. S. 1984. "Toward an Holistic View of Persons with Learning Disabilities." In *Learning Disability Quarterly,* 7, 4: 290–294.

———. 1988a. "The Reductionistic Fallacy in Learning Disabilities: Replicating the Past by Reducing the Present." In *Journal of Learning Disabilities,* 21: 389–400.

———. 1988b. "Holistic/Constructivist Principles of the Teaching/Learning Process: Implications for the Field of Learning Disabilities." In *Journal of Learning Disabilities,* 21: 401–416.

Randolph, M. K., and G. R. Gridler. 1985. "Children of Divorce." In *Technique,* 1: 166–175.

Read, C. 1975. *Children's Categorizations of Speech Sounds in English.* Urbana, IL: National Council of Teachers of English.

Reid, D. K., W. P. Hresko, and D. D. Hammill. 1989. *Test of Early Reading Ability-2.* Austin, TX: PRO-Ed.

Rhodes, L. K., and C. Dudley-Marling. 1988. *Readers and Writers with a Difference.* Portsmouth, NH: Heinemann.

Rogers, J. 1993. "The Inclusion Revolution." In *Phi Delta Kappa Research Bulletin,* 11: 1–6.

Salvia, J., and J. E. Ysseldyke. 1981. *Assessment in Special and Remedial Education.* Boston: Houghton Mifflin.

Samway, K. D., G. Whang, and M. Pippitt. 1995. *Buddy Reading.* Portsmouth, NH: Heinemann.

Schleper, D. R., and M. Farmer. 1991. "An Interdisciplinary Approach to Applying Recent Research in Literacy in the Education of Hearing Impaired, Learning Disabled Students." U.S. Department of Education Teacher/Researcher Grant #R11780077.

Searfoss, L. W. 1994. "A Holitic/Wellness Model of Reading Assessment: An Alternative to the Medical Model." In *Reading & Writing Quarterly: Overcoming Learning Difficulties,* 10: 103–117.

Sendak, M. 1963. *Where the Wild Things Are.* New York: Scholastic.

Sharan, S. J. 1980. "Cooperative Learning in Small Groups: Recent Methods and Effects on Achievement, Attitudes and Ethnic Relations." In *Review of Educational Research,* 50: 241–249.

Shepard, L. A. 1987. "The New Push for Excellence: Widening the Schism Between Regular and Special Education." In *Exceptional Children,* 53: 327–329.

Sippola, A. E. 1995. "K-W-L-S." In *The Reading Teacher,* 48: 542–543.

Sitton, R., and R. Forest. 1987. *The Quick-Word Handbook for Everyday Writers.* North Billerica, MA: Curriculum Associates.

Slavin, R. E. 1983. *Cooperative Learning.* White Plains, NY: Longman.

———. 1990. *Cooperative Learning: Theory, Research, and Practice.* Englewood Cliffs, NJ: Prentice Hall.

Smith, F. 1971. *Understanding Reading.* New York: Holt, Rinehart, and Winston.

———. 1982. *Understanding Reading* 3d ed. New York: Holt, Rinehart, and Winston.

———. 1983. *Essays into Literacy.* Portsmouth, NH: Heinemann.

———. 1985. *Reading Without Nonsense.* New York: Teachers College Press.

Smith, S. 1990. "Comparison of Individualized Education Programs (IEPs) of Students with Behavioral Disorders and Learning Disabilities." In *The Journal of Special Education,* 24: 85–99.

Stainback, S., and W. Stainback. 1984. "A Rationale for the Merger of Special and Regular Education." In *Exceptional Children,* 51: 101–111.

———. 1992. "Schools in Inclusive Communities." In *Controversial Issues Confronting Special Education.* W. Stainback and S. Stainback, eds. Needham Heights, MA: Allyn & Bacon.

Stake, R. E. 1975. *Evaluating the Arts in Education: A Responsive Approach.* Columbus, OH: Merrill.

Stevens, R. J., and R. E. Slavin. 1992. *The Cooperative Elementary School: Effects on Students' Achievement, Attitudes and Social Relations.* Baltimore, MD: Center for Research on Effective Schooling for Disadvantaged Students.

Stice, C., and N. Bertrand. 1989. "The Texts and Texture of Literacy Learning in Whole Language Versus Traditional/Skills Classrooms." In *National Reading Conference Yearbook.* S. McCormick and J. Zutell, eds.

Sullivan, M. W., and M. Lewis. 1990. "Contingency Intervention: A Program Portrait." In *Journal of Early Intervention,* 14, 4: 367–375.

Sumner, H. 1993. "Whole Language Assessment and Evaluation: A Special Education Perspective." In *Assessment and Evaluation in Whole Language Programs.* B. Harp, ed. Norwood, MA: Christopher-Gordon.

Taylor, N. E., I. H. Blum, and D. M. Logsdon. 1986. "The Development of Written Language Awareness: Environmental Aspects and Program Characteristics." In *Reading Research Quarterly,* 21: 132–149.

Trelease, J. 1989. "Jim Trelease Speaks on Reading Aloud to Children." In *The Reading Teacher,* 43, 3: 200–206.

Tunnell, M. O., and J. S. Jacobs. 1989. "Using 'Real' Books: Research Findings on Literature Based Reading Instruction." In *Reading Teacher,* 42, 7: 470–477.

Turbill, J. 1983. *Now, We Want to Write!* Rozelle, NSW: Primary English Teaching Association. Distributed by Heinemann, Portsmouth, NH.

Valencia, S. W., and P. D. Pearson. 1988. "Principles for Classroom Comprehension Assessment." In *Remedial and Special Education,* 9: 26–35.

Venn, J. 1994. *Assessment of Students with Special Needs.* New York: Merrill.

Viorst, J. 1972. *Alexander and the Terrible, Horrible, No Good, Very Bad Day.* New York: Macmillan.

Vygotsky, L. S. 1978. *Mind in Society: The Development of Higher Psychological Processes.* M. Cole, V. J. Steiner, S. Scribbner, and E. Souberman, eds. Cambridge, MA: Harvard University Press.

Walker, B. J. 1992. *Supporting Struggling Readers.* Markham, ONT: Pippin.

Wells, G. 1980. *Learning Through Interaction.* Cambridge, UK: Cambridge University Press.

Wheat, L. B. 1932. "Four Spelling Rules." In *Elementary School Journal,* 32: 697–706.

Wilde, S. 1989. "Looking at Invented Spelling: A Kid Watcher's Guide to Spelling, Part 1." In *The Whole Language Evaluation Book.* K. S. Goodman, Y. M. Goodman, and W. J. Hood, eds. Portsmouth, NH: Heinemann.

————. 1990. "A Proposal for a New Spelling Curriculum." In *The Elementary School Journal,* 90, 3: 275–289.

Will, M. C. 1986. "Education Children with Learning Problems: A Shared Responsibility." In *Exceptional Children,* 53: 411–415.

Winsor, P. J., and P. D. Pearson. 1992. *Children at Risk: Their Phonemic Awareness Development in Holistic Instruction* (Report No. CSR-TR-556). Urbana, IL: Center for the Study of Reading. (ERIC Document Reproduction Service No. ED 345 209).

Wortis, S., and L. Hall. 1990. "Infusing Multiculturalism in a Whole Language Classroom." In *The Whole Language Teachers Association Newsletter,* 5, 2: 1–4.

Yellen, D., and M. E. Blake. 1994. *Integrating Language Arts: A Holistic Approach.* New York: HarperCollins.

Index